$\mathcal{G}$ eorge turned her head to follow Mary's gaze. Bronson was standing at the hostess desk scanning the room. His face lit up as their eyes met. He made a beeline for their table. "George! Kim told me she thought you'd be here."

"Hello, Bronson," Mary interjected.

"Hi, Mary," he said, but his eyes were only for Georgine. "I was at the Far East office this morning to debrief about my last trip. While I was there, twenty-three assignments came in. George, you have a baby!"

She was out of her seat and in his arms almost before his words were out. She'd known the moment she saw his face something wonderful had happened. Bronson didn't get excited for nothing.

"Everyone's looking," he teased, his mouth against her ear as she hugged him, laughing and crying at the same time.

"Let them look." She pulled away, flinging one arm out as she held tightly to his hand with the other, and announced to the entire dining room, "I'm getting a baby!"

Other Palisades by Barbara Jean Hicks:

Coming Home
Snow Swan

novellas in
Mistletoe
Heart's Delight

China doll

BARBARA JEAN HICKS

PALISADES

This is a work of fiction. The characters, incidents, and dialogues are products of the author's imagination and are not to be construed as real. Any resemblance to actual events or persons, living or dead, is entirely coincidental.

CHINA DOLL
published by Palisades
a division of Multnomah Publishers, Inc.

© 1998 by Barbara Jean Hicks
International Standard Book Number: 1–57673–262–2

Cover illustration by Paul Bachem
Design by Brenda McGee

Printed in the United States of America

For information:
MULTNOMAH PUBLISHERS, INC.•POST OFFICE BOX 1720
SISTERS, OREGON 97759

Library of Congress Cataloging-in-Publication Data:
Hicks, Barbara Jean.
China doll / by Barbara Jean Hicks.
    p. cm.
ISBN 1–57673–262–2 (alk. paper)
I. Title.
PS3558.I22976C48   1998   98–5550
    813'.54—dc21   CIP

98 99 00 01 02 03 04 — 10 9 8 7 6 5 4 3 2 1

With love and gratitude to my parents,
Charlotte and Irby Hicks,
whose heart for children is my legacy.

ACKNOWLEDGMENTS

Special thanks to JP Christy and Lisa Dubitsky, for making connections; to Pauline Pennell and Mary Wilson for insight into catalog production; to Michael Han for information about Chinese culture and adoption from China; and especially to Pat Golbieski, Kim Lathrop, and Beau Luque, for sharing so freely your adoption stories and your beautiful daughters, Jet Chun Mei and Maya Chan Wei. May your love and courage inspire others as they have inspired me.

*Delight yourself in the L*ORD
and he will give you the desires of your heart.

P**SALM** 37:4

Prologue

Yin Zhaodi sat near a window in the main wing of the sprawling house where Mother Hu held court, silent among the chattering of the other women, her quick, capable fingers pushing and pulling the needle through the red silk which fell across her rounded belly.

When she finished the embroidery, five bats would fly across the tiny gown, symbols of the five blessings she wished for the child in her womb: long life, riches, tranquillity, a love of virtue, a good end.

The baby gave a sudden kick. Zhaodi's flash of joy was just as sudden. *I love you, little one.*

Exhilaration flooded through her veins. Tonight was the night. The eve of a new year. The eve of a new life…

On the bench next to her, Fourth Sister stopped her mending and leaned over to stroke the fabric. "Ah—such fine quality!" she said. "Excellent silk. Exceptional needlework." She smiled. "You make a full-month gown worthy of a little emperor."

Zhaodi glanced quickly at her sister-in-law, pleased. Emboldened by her husband's conviction that she carried a son, she had asked him for red cotton to make a gown for the baby's full-month feast and yellow cotton to line it. He had returned from the district capital one day with red and yellow silk.

"You are kind to say so, Sister."

"Tianqing is treating you well?" Fourth Sister asked, her voice low.

She nodded. "For now. He wishes health for his unborn son." Of all the women in the household, Fourth Sister alone knew about the bruises Zhaodi hid beneath the long sleeves of her tunic. And even she had never seen the stripes across Zhaodi's back.

"Ah. Perhaps he will respect you more as mother of his son," Fourth Sister said.

Zhaodi concentrated on her flying fingers. "Perhaps," she said. Her voice gave nothing away.

Early in Zhaodi's pregnancy, Mother Hu had declared with authority, "I have checked the *Sheng Nan Yu Nü de Yuce Biao*. Praise to the gods, you will have a boy!"

Zhaodi had less faith in the Prediction Chart for Birthing Boys and Bearing Girls, based as it was on peasant superstition, but she did not argue. For now, Tianqing's belief she carried his son was her only protection.

And if it should be a girl she carried? Zhaodi knew that neither she nor her child would survive Tianqing's wrath if she bore him a daughter instead of a son.

A baby girl was lucky to survive in China, she told herself as she knotted the thread and cut it with her teeth. The government's one-child policy saw to that. Who wanted a worthless girl as their only child? Unwanted pregnancies were dealt with.

And unwanted births.

The stories were common gossip about the house and in the village: this father who had drowned his daughter at birth, that mother who had smothered her infant girl. One couple who had buried their female child alive to make way for a son.

Other parents, only slightly more compassionate, left their daughters in the hands of fate by the sides of busy roads, in front of police stations, on the steps of overcrowded orphanages....

Tianqing would not stand for a daughter.

Becoming his wife had been too easy, Zhaodi thought. Her younger brother had been anxious to have her out of the house, to make room for a wife and a son to carry on the family name. Tianqing was tall and strong, from a good family who had supported the revolution. Zhaodi had been flattered and honored at his attentions. The marriage was arranged without her protest.

How could she have known? Her own father had been strict and taciturn but treated her mother with respect. Was that not what a husband did?

Soon enough she found that it was not—at least for Tianqing. At first she was too shocked at his abuse to speak of it to anyone. Later, she was too afraid. Finally she accepted her fate and resolved to endure her husband's cruelty however she could.

How can an egg break a rock? she would tell herself. *What can I do?* To leave him would be to lose face for herself and her family. Besides, where would she go?

Tianqing berated her for her submission even as he battered her. "You *ask* me to beat you, old hen!" he shouted. "You do not even fight me!" And then, with contempt, "You have no liver at all!" *No courage.*

For three years Zhaodi had been an obedient servant and compliant wife. But seven months ago, when she first learned that she carried the seed of a child in her belly, everything changed.

On the outside she remained submissive, but on the inside, her love for the child she carried burned away the fear her husband had instilled. Her love for her baby made her strong. *Do not wake the sleeping tiger, Tianqing,* she warned him in her mind.

She had never felt such fierce protectiveness. She could feel her liver growing larger every day. No matter what, she would not let her husband harm her child.

The baby gave another kick inside her womb. She placed a hand against her belly, smiling faintly. *Boy or girl, you will live,* she said in her mind. *Soon, you and I will be gone from this house and this village forever.*

For six months she had perfected her plans. She knew when she would leave, what she would take with her, where she would go, how she would get there. After that—her life was in the hands of fate.

Fate could never be as cruel, she thought, as was Tianqing.

And tonight was the night of her leaving. This new-moon night which ended an old year and began a new one also ended her old life and began a new one.

No more a wife, but soon a mother. Her unborn child was getting restless. The baby would push its way into the world before the next dark moon.

Yes, tonight was the night of her leaving. No one would see her go, hours ahead and in the opposite direction of her much discussed visit to her widowed mother up the mountain, three villages away.

So gracious was Mother Hu, her sisters-in-law murmured, allowing Zhaodi to spend a part of Spring Festival with her old mother! Such a thoughtful husband was Tianqing to let her go!

Zhaodi knew the truth: that after the fireworks Tianqing would leave for the next village to be with the mistress he had taken when his wife's belly had grown "unsightly."

She had been careful not to give herself away. As the new year approached, she kept tradition as she had every year of her marriage, cleaning their rooms from top to bottom to sweep away the bad luck of the old year and make way for good luck in the new, giving fresh coats of paint to the door and window frames—red, for happiness and good fortune. Helping Mother Hu and her sisters-in-law prepare the new year's feast days in advance: *fatsai,* black-hair fungus, to soak up good fortune; sun-dried oysters to invite wealth; fast-cooked shrimp to ensure laughter and happiness; *jiaozi,* New Year dumplings, to ensure the birth of sons.

Her most difficult task in those last days had been hiding her contempt for Tianqing, pretending his demands did not disgust her. Only for the sake of her child had she been able to bring herself to rub his feet, scratch his back, prepare his favorite meals, say nothing when he stayed away all night and came back reeking of another woman.

The family feast on the eve of the new year was noisy with commotion. Even Tianqing was in good spirits, telling stories that made everyone laugh. Only once, when Fourth Sister reached over to squeeze Zhaodi's hand, did she feel a moment of sadness. If Tianqing had loved her, she might have been happy here. If he loved her, he would love their child, boy or girl.

But he did not love her. Zhaodi hardened her heart, even against Fourth Sister, whom she knew would not stand up for her against Tianqing if it came to that.

After the tables were cleared, she excused herself to lie down for an hour before the evening revelry began. "The baby," she apologized, needing no other reason. In the room she had shared for three years with Tianqing, she quickly gathered together the few items she would take with her.

Her heart beat faster as she felt the edges of the twenty *yuan* sewn into the lining of her cloth handbag. What she had saved would not go far, but she would have enough left after the long bus ride from the district capital to Fuzhou to pay her old friend Li Jing Mei for food and lodging until her baby was born. After that…

Something would work out. She would find a job. Maybe in the child welfare agency where Jing Mei worked, or in one of the many factories. Maybe in one of the large hotels where foreigners stayed…

She had not written Jing Mei of her coming; she could not afford the risk. But she had her old friend's address in the city. She would find her. And Jing Mei would not let her down.

Zhaodi returned to the main wing of the sprawling house just as Second Sister was gathering the children on the floor around her for the telling of the traditional new-year's tale. Lowering herself to the wooden bench against the wall, her hands supporting her belly, she settled in and listened quietly.

"Long ago," the storyteller began, "when the eldest of our eldest ancestors tilled the land on the hillsides where our rice and vegetables grow, every year on the eve of the new year coming a monstrous beast would roam the earth from end to end, seeking people to devour. His name was Nian, and he had long, sharp teeth and a mouth as hungry as the sea, a mouth that could swallow whole villages in one gigantic gulp.

"One year, near the end of the season of Great Cold as the new year approached, a very wise and fearless old man walked to meet the beast outside our village—" Second Sister stopped, flinging her arm toward the window—"just there, down the road!"

Their eyes wide with excitement, the children at her feet glanced toward the window.

"What happened? What happened?" Zhaodi's eldest nephew demanded, bouncing with impatience, as if he had never heard the tale before.

"Ah! The beast roared! And gnashed his teeth! And prepared to devour this foolish human! But—" The storyteller raised her hand. "When the old man raised his hand, just so, Nian stopped. Perhaps he was curious to know why this human did not turn and try to run away as all the others had.

"Whatever the reason, Nian spared the old man's life and listened to his words. 'I have heard it said from one end of the earth to the other what a grand hunter you are,' the old man told the creature. 'Ferocious, terrible, fearing nothing. Surely puny humans are unworthy opponents for such a great hunter as you!' he said. 'Would it not be more sporting to pursue the beasts of prey which roam the earth?'

"And so on that night before the new year, the monster left the villagers alone and roamed the earth instead, and did the villagers a great service by devouring many hundreds of beasts of prey, ridding the world of them forever!

"And while he was gone, the old man told the villagers that though the beast seemed fearless, there was one thing he was afraid of—the color red. 'Decorate your doors and windows with red paper at each year's end, and you will frighten the beast away for another circling of the seasons,' he said. 'Every year you must remember to do this, and Nian will never bother you again.'

"The monster, having had his fill of wild beasts, returned to our village a docile creature. And then, to everyone's surprise, the old man jumped up on his back and rode away! He was not an old man at all, you see, but an immortal god who had taken pity on the people."

The storyteller scanned the faces glued to her own. "We have painted our doors and windows red and decorated them with red paper as the old man instructed," she said. "What else must we do to frighten away the monster Nian on this eve of the new year?"

"Firecrackers!" the children shouted in unison, scrambling up from their positions on the floor and leaping with excitement.

"Firecrackers!" Second Sister echoed. *"Guo Nian,* children!"

"Guo Nian!" they shouted back.

"Guo Nian," repeated Zhaodi softly. "Happy New Year! Beast, pass over our house...."

But for Zhaodi, the beast was here, inside the house.

It was time to go.

One

*D*ear Uncle Bron, the e-mail message read. *Thanks for all the neat stuff you sent me about Hong Kong! I got an A+ on my school report!! When are you coming to Portland? It would be way cool if you spoke in my class!!! Then maybe my friend Danny would believe in you. Your FRIEND (and niece), Isabel Lewis.*

Bronson Bailey laughed out loud at the exuberance of his niece's message. Six exclamation points—not a record for Izzy, but a substantial number for five sentences.

He clicked on the Reply icon and typed in, *Dear Isabel— You're welcome. Congratulations on the report—maybe you inherited some of your Uncle Bron's talent!*

She even had *him* using exclamation points, he thought wryly—punctuation he used sparingly if at all in the news and feature articles he wrote for a living.

But lavishly in real life, he'd been told. From hang gliding off ocean cliffs as a teenager to volunteering for active duty in Vietnam to dodging bullets in other war zones as a foreign correspondent, Bronson had always sought excitement. Maybe it was in his genes. Maybe it was a reaction to growing up a small-town preacher's kid on the Oregon coast. Maybe it was the influence of his mother's sister, Lydia Bronson—a feeling he had to live up to the name they shared.

He wondered how Aunt Liddy was doing. In her nineties now, she still lived independently in her house overlooking the Pacific, a house with a Chinese garden she called *Xi Jia Lou*, House of Evening Splendor. A place where Bronson had spent many hours of his growing-up years listening to his aunt's stories about life in China.

Aunt Liddy had lived and worked in The Middle Kingdom as a missionary nurse and midwife during a time of great political and social upheaval, through the Sino-Japanese War and then the bitter civil war between Mao's Red Army and Chiang Kai-shek's nationalist party, the Kuomintang. Her tales had kept him on the edge of his seat when he was a boy, wide-eyed with awe, and later inspired his advanced degree in Asian studies and his desire to live and work in the Far East.

She hadn't yet answered his last letter, mailed probably a month ago. Too bad his aunt wasn't plugged into the Internet like her great-niece was....

If your friend Danny has problems believing I'm for real, he added to his e-mail message, *you should tell him about your Great-aunt Liddy. You'll really have him rolling his eyes in disbelief.*

As to the question Izzy posed about a visit to Portland...

He wondered if Mary had put her daughter up to that.

Bronson had never been entirely comfortable around his sister and her husband Mark—"Chappie," as he was called at the large church where he was college minister. He and Mary couldn't have made more different choices for their lives. All those kids! Seven, plus at least a couple of grandkids by now.

I probably won't get to Portland for a while, he typed. *But keep in touch. You never know.* He signed off, then clicked the icon that would send the message into cyberspace for his niece to retrieve.

Long ago, as a restless and ambitious young journalist, Bronson had made a conscious choice to commit himself to the demands of his career instead of settling down with a wife and raising a family. At first he hadn't wanted to take the time and energy away from his work. But after twenty years of focusing on hard news stories about man's inhumanity to man, he wondered how anyone could justify bringing children into the world. Even more, how anyone could bear watching children grow up in such a world....

Bronson didn't regret his decision to forgo family.

Yet sometimes he felt very alone.

Maybe he should marry Pamela. Maybe it was finally time to settle down—not roses-climbing-over-a-white-picket-fence settling down, definitely not children-bouncing-on-their-adoring-daddy's-knee settling down. Just...

Someone to meet him at the airport when he came home from assignment would be nice, he thought. Someone he knew would be there for him when he needed her.

He knew he didn't live the kind of life most women would be interested in sharing with a man. But he and Pamela had been friends for half a dozen years. Dated some, though mostly on a casual basis; they tacitly agreed that work came first for both of them. Pamela understood him, knew she couldn't tie him down. Marriage to her would be comfortable. Convenient. All the perks and none of the demands...

He was glad she wanted to see him tonight; it had been too long. Reaching for the phone, he punched in a number stored in memory. Two rings and an answering machine clicked on.

"Pamela—Bronson. Just confirming dinner tonight. I'll pick you up at seven. Want to tag along with me later while I track down the rest of the story I'm working on? Expect travel at the speed of light and a very quick kiss good-night—I have a dozen street corners to hit and a 2 A.M. deadline. Let me know."

He browsed through the rest of his e-mail, dumping the advertising, saving several dispatches from Beijing, Taipei, and Tokyo, and answering the message from his editor in Los

Angeles about his current assignment, a feature on the first Chinese New Year celebration in Hong Kong since the British had returned the protectorate to China. Because of the time difference, he'd be able to roam the streets tonight, add the finishing touches to his story after the midnight fireworks, and get it to Stan for inclusion in tomorrow's afternoon edition of the *Los Angeles Examiner* before the West Coast celebrations of the holiday kicked in.

He spent the rest of the day writing up the research he'd already done for the article, historical information on the lunar new year and interviews with various Chinese officials about their perspective on this year's celebration. Tonight after his man-on-the-street interviews, he'd add his own impressions of the spirit of Hong Kong's first truly Chinese New Year in over a hundred and fifty years.

It was the kind of article he'd once have been impatient having to write, a "soft" news story. No real significance or weight. After his last major assignment, however, the Chinese New Year feature was a welcome relief. The series of articles he'd researched and written about baby girls "gone missing" in the People's Republic of China had shaken him badly.

His sense of relief for the soft assignment disturbed him. Was he going soft himself? Is that what this sudden sense of loneliness was about?

Pamela had once suggested he was "too much in touch with the world and not in touch enough with himself." In his work, it was called "journalistic objectivity" and considered a good thing.

But this story...

It might have been different if the missing baby girls he'd written about were an anomaly in China. They weren't. Literally millions of girls were unaccounted for over the almost twenty years since the government had imposed its strict population control policies across the country.

He'd interviewed no-nonsense population control workers, dour policemen, and politely evasive child welfare officers in several cities. He'd visited a dozen orphanages, some where the staff was doing a decent job under trying conditions to care for their charges, and others where he'd witnessed unbelievable and even deadly neglect.

He'd also talked to dozens of people who "knew someone" who'd killed or abandoned an infant daughter—though he'd found no one who admitted to having done such a thing himself. It was, after all, against the law.

Never had his journalistic objectivity felt so compromised. He had not been able to stay detached.

He arrived at Pamela's high-rise apartment a few minutes before seven and rang the bell outside her door on the twenty-sixth floor exactly on the hour. She didn't answer immediately; he rang again.

"Bronson?"

"Yes."

"Hang on."

She'd called this afternoon to decline his invitation to tag along while he chased his story, which surprised him a little; Pamela was usually game for anything. She'd been traveling a lot, she said. She was tired.

He buried his hands in the pockets of his chinos, head down, as she slid back the dead bolt and chain and swung the door inward.

She was wearing a silk robe in vibrant hues, red and green and blue flowers splashed across a black background, and her head was wrapped in a white towel. "I wish you hadn't been so punctual," she said, not embarrassed, not irritated, just telling the truth.

He raised his eyebrows. Even without makeup she was beautiful, her features just irregular enough not to be ordinary, her skin smooth, her blue eyes fringed with heavy lashes. A tall, leggy blonde with brains, money, and ambition to boot. A woman who understood him. If he'd had an ounce of sense, he'd have asked her to marry him years ago.

"You're not ready." He kissed her lightly.

"I'm sorry." She turned away. There was something cool and formal and distant about her, even here in her own home, dressed in her robe with her hair wrapped in a towel.

"I got tied up on the phone," she said. "A drink?"

"I'll get it." He hesitated. "Everything all right?"

He couldn't interpret the look she gave him, the quick lift of her head, the direct blue gaze that suddenly slid away and left him feeling somehow stranded, standing there in the middle of her beautifully appointed apartment.

Stranded—it was a good word to describe the way he'd been feeling lately. Disconnected. Restless. Not his customary action-verb exclamatory-sentence restlessness, something different. Since finishing the "Gone Missing" series, he'd even found himself asking unanswerable philosophical questions: *Who am I? What am I doing here?*

When he'd mentioned his growing restlessness to his editor at the *Los Angeles Examiner* in an overseas phone call a month before, Stan hadn't made the connection between the series Bronson was working on and his state of mind. Bronson himself wasn't sure there was a connection.

"How old are you?" Stan asked him instead.

"Forty-nine."

"A little old for a midlife crisis, but you've got the symptoms," Stan declared, as if he was an authority on the subject. "Watch out, Bailey."

"I thought midlife crises happened to married men with 2.2 children, a house in the suburbs, two cars in the garage, and a midmanagement job in corporate America."

"They happen to bachelor guys like you, too. Only instead of trading in the wife for a red Ferrari, bachelors trade in the Ferrari for a wife."

It was significant that Bronson hadn't dismissed Stan's pronouncement out of hand. What if the old buzzard knew what he was talking about?

He reached for Pamela. "You're beautiful," he murmured.

She placed a hand on his chest, preventing the embrace, and gave him that same unreadable look. "I'll be ready in half an hour. Make yourself at home," she said, and left him.

Bronson used the phone to change their dinner reservations, gazing out the floor-to-ceiling windows over the city below. Hong Kong. Bright lights and promises—the brightest lights and the loudest, most outrageous promises of any city he'd ever known. She pulsated with energy, a living, breathing creature—neon flashing, horns blaring, heat rising from the streets. And money braying like a hawker in the marketplace. Every dream for sale, in English and Chinese alike.

She was an impossible city, he thought as he clicked off the portable phone. Always had been. A paean to unrestrained capitalism sitting on the back stoop of the largest Communist nation in the world.

Most observers were cautiously optimistic about the future now that Britain's lease on the protectorate had expired. True, a number of international corporations had relocated in the years preceding the British pullout, anticipating problems. And the stock market had been all over the charts in the past few months. But the People's Republic of China knew a good thing when they had it. Bronson couldn't help but believe Beijing was going to do everything in its power to retain Hong Kong's leadership in the world economy.

The lights were almost hypnotic. He'd forgotten how spectacular the view was from Pamela's apartment. How long had it been since he'd looked out these windows?

"Three months," she answered from the other room when he called out the question. "I've added to my collection, by the way. Did you notice?"

Three months! He'd been neglecting her. And hadn't even realized it. Was that why she'd turned down his invitation to explore the city for his Chinese New Year story after dinner? She had a right to be disgruntled.

He moved to examine her collection, displayed in sleek mahogany cabinets along one wall of the living room: museum-quality porcelain from China's last imperial dynasty, the Qing. The few pieces represented a small fortune. Pamela had *earned* a small fortune in the last ten years, selling her company's engineering services to the Chinese government. Did the officials she worked with think it was a fair trade-off? Dams and highways for small pieces of history? The future for the past?

The porcelain was exquisite: A delicate moon flask, decorated in cobalt blue and white with a songbird on a branch of flowering plum. A deeply foliated bowl on a base—a sunflower bowl, he remembered, decorated with elegant Chinese ladies in a garden. A pair of graceful *meiping* vases, one with peonies and a colorful rooster, the other with lotus and a pair of ducks. Mandarin ducks—a traditional symbol for marital bliss. He stared at the vase for a long moment, lost in thought, before moving on.

Pamela's newest piece was a plate with an elaborate floral and geometric border and a detailed scene of a seated woman with two young boys playing at her feet. A woman who had justified her existence by producing sons. Only in modern China, she would have been allowed to bear only one....

"I've been looking for that plate for years," Pamela said, startling him from his reverie. He watched her as she clipped on diamond earrings and walked toward him. Her dress, cut close and slim, was the same blue as her eyes.

I'm going to ask her, Bronson suddenly resolved. *Tonight.*

"Recognize the *famille rose* palette?" she asked.

He was looking at her, not the plate. "Remind me."

Her explanation was lost on him; her perfume was too distracting. He put an arm around her waist.

She lifted it off and continued as if she didn't know she was driving him crazy. "The new opaque white could be blended with the traditional washes to create pastels. Look how much more delicate the lines and colors are...."

"Stop talking, Pamela," he murmured, pulling her toward him.

"Bronson—" She pushed away from his embrace.

He let go, surprised.

"I need to tell you something." She walked to the windows, gazing out over the city for a long moment. When she turned, he knew suddenly what she was going to say.

"I'm getting married."

He stopped breathing. *Getting married.* Pamela was getting married!

It doesn't matter, he told himself. *I'm not in love with her.* But if he wasn't in love with her, why did he feel as if the wind had been knocked out of him? Why did he feel so desolate?

"I'd thought you might consider marrying me," he blurted,

hardly realizing what he said.

She laughed. "Yeah, right."

His breath released on a long sigh. She wasn't taking him seriously. With good reason, he thought, his eyes still holding hers across the room. In all the years they'd known each other, marriage had never been a consideration.

He didn't want to marry her now. Not really. He'd been lonely, and a little intoxicated by her beauty. Something was missing in his life, and he'd thought for a moment it was Pamela.

He wondered what she saw in his eyes.

"Bronson..." she said, then shook her head and turned her gaze back toward the window. Was it sadness that colored her voice?

"I've always known you weren't the marrying kind," she said. She slanted another look at him. "You've got that journalistic objectivity down so pat you wouldn't know how to get your heart involved if you wanted to."

But I don't have it down pat, he wanted to protest. *And I do want to get my heart involved....*

He reached for her wrap, draped across the back of the sofa. It was too late to say anything like that.

Walking up behind her, he settled it over her shoulders, smoothed it down her arms.

"So who's the lucky man?" he asked lightly.

Two

"H ey, George!"

Georgine Nichols looked up from the drafting table where she was working, her back to the view of the Portland skyline across the Willamette River. She peered over her reading glasses at the athletic young woman striding through the doorway into her office.

"Congrats!" Hadley said, holding up a copy of the new spring catalog in one hand and raising her other hand to slap Georgine's in an exuberant high-five. "Another winner!"

A pretty Asian woman, her fall of shiny dark hair swinging against her shoulders, followed Hadley into the office and seated herself at the oversized desk that sat at an angle to Georgine's. Her assistant, Kim Horton, dropped her large handbag on the desk, looking at her boss with obvious admiration. "No surprise," she said.

Georgine raised her eyebrows. "As if you had nothing to do with it, Kim," she said. Then, turning back to Hadley, "Thanks—we kind of like it ourselves!"

She was pleased with the spring catalog, especially the cover, which featured her favorite photo from their September shoot in San Diego: a curly-haired toddler in floral-printed overalls from the PlayLittles line, sitting in the dirt among overturned clay pots and digging with a spade, her tongue caught between her teeth in a look of utter concentration. Such focus!

George especially loved the fact that the little girl's knees were soiled. One of the distinctives she'd created for the Child's

Play catalogs was an impression in the photographs of real children engaged in real play.

She was proud of the advertising awards her catalogs had garnered, but they didn't mean as much as the awards several of her photos had won in juried shows. Even when the intention of her photography was advertising, she always approached her camera work as art.

"How's the mailing going?" she asked Hadley.

"Getting 'em out. Got a couple of *great* guys from the temp agency," the shipping supervisor said, her short brown curls bouncing as she nodded her head for emphasis. Her eyes gleamed with mischief. "And *very* cute. Better go check on 'em. See you!"

Kim Horton shook her head as Hadley bounded away. "I'll be glad when softball season rolls around," she said. "That girl needs to run off some energy."

Georgine sighed and stretched. "Would that I still had as much."

"You mean you *did* at some point? I'm the same age as Hadley, and I've *never* had that much energy," Kim said dryly.

"I forget what a young thing you are." George eyed her assistant. "Funny, isn't it? I think of Hadley as barely past adolescence, but I consider you my peer."

"If it weren't for the fact you're pushing forty, I'd feel complimented," Kim teased.

"Oh, sure, rub it in," Georgine huffed in pretended injury. She didn't mind Kim's teasing. Despite the laugh lines etched at the corners of her eyes and mouth and the reading glasses she suddenly couldn't do without, she felt good, and she knew she looked good for a woman "pushing forty." She'd been blessed with good genes, she supposed. And she tried to take care of herself, though regular exercise was getting harder and harder to fit into her crazy schedule.

And she'd thought freelancing had been hectic.

As creative director for Child's Play, a mail-order children's clothing company she'd helped organize three years earlier, Georgine handled the design and production of four catalogs a year, as well as much of the photography between their covers.

Kim had been her assistant since the beginning, fresh out of college with a degree in literature she'd feared would make her unmarketable. To the contrary, her liberal arts background had stood out in the stack of business and technology résumés George had read through. Kim was bright, organized, detail-oriented, and by this time could almost read her boss's mind.

As if to illustrate the point, she answered the question George hadn't yet asked. "Found the perfect location for the fall catalog shoot today," she said, pulling out of her handbag a Polaroid camera and a manila envelope. She tossed the envelope to Georgine as she deposited the camera in a desk drawer.

"It's Bybee Elementary School, in Eastmoreland," she explained as Georgine shuffled through the prints she'd pulled from the envelope. "A great old brick building with white-painted trim. Fresh blacktop on the playground, with newly painted hopscotch squares and basketball keys. Tether ball, a couple of interesting climbing structures, a ball field—what d' you think?"

"Hmm…looks promising," George answered as she skimmed through the pictures a second time. The management team had chosen a school recess theme for the fall catalog, and Kim had been out scouting locations all week. "Have you checked with the school district yet about permissions?"

Kim looked at her watch. "First thing Monday," she promised. Closing her handbag, she stood and slung it across her shoulder. "Meantime, I'm outta here. Spencer's talked me

into hanging out in Chinatown for the Chinese New Year celebration tonight." She hesitated. "Care to join us?"

"Thanks, but no. I've got a baby shower tonight." Besides,
Kim and Spencer had just started dating; she wasn't interested
in making "company" a "crowd."

The phone rang. Georgine waved her assistant out the door.
"I'll get it. Have fun!" She reached for the receiver.

"Child's Play, Georgine."

"Hi, George. It's Mary."

"Hi!" She used her shoulder to hold the receiver to her ear,
freeing her hands to lay Kim's photos out across the drafting
table. "Still want me to pick you up tonight?" she asked her
friend.

"Actually, there's been a change of plans. Katie couldn't wait
for us, I guess. Or at least the baby couldn't."

"She had her baby!"

"This morning. A boy. Eight pounds, six ounces."

"A bruiser!" Georgine pulled several photos toward her
from the lineup. Definite possibilities. "So the shower's off?"

"No—Katie's feeling great, so Emily and Toni decided to
have the shower in her room at the hospital. Emanuel. That's
on your side of town, so I'll go ahead and drive myself. Isabel
wants to come, too, believe it or not. Even has a dress picked
out to wear. Maybe there's a girlie-girl inside that tomboy after
all."

Izzy was twelve, and one of Georgine's favorite kids. "Don't
wish too hard for a girlie-girl. I think tomboys have an easier
time of adolescence."

Mary groaned. "*No* one has an easy time of adolescence. Six
down and Izzy to go. Did you have to remind me?"

Georgine laughed. "You know you love every last minute of
motherhood, Mary." She collected the photos spread across the

table and slipped them back in the envelope. Maybe she'd drive out this weekend to see the school herself. "So I'll see you at Emanuel, then. Seven? Sounds fun!"

Fun turned out to be the wrong word altogether. Almost from the moment she walked into the maternity ward at the hospital later that evening, Georgine knew it had been a mistake to come.

First there was the nursery. She couldn't keep herself from standing at the window in the hallway and watching as a nurse picked up a squalling, red-faced baby and held it in her arms, rocking gently to soothe its tears. She winced at the sound of its wailing cry, feeling it almost as physical pain, like an arrow piercing her heart. Another baby joined the first, as if in empathy. George winced again, the pain sharper.

Turning, she walked resolutely toward the nurse's station, clutching her brightly-wrapped shower gift as if she were afraid someone might snatch it away.

"Katie Castle?" she inquired at the reception desk.

The young woman behind the counter smiled. "You're here for the shower. Mother and child doing fine, Room 2509." She pointed down the hallway.

George's steps slowed as she approached the room. Maybe she should leave now, before anyone knew she was here. She could always say something had come up at work. She could always take her gift to church on Sunday....

"Georgine! In here!"

Too late.

Mary gave her a hug as she entered the room. "Hi, Mary." But her eyes went straight to Katie, sitting up in bed, gazing down at the bundle in her arms.

She was radiant, the wisps of auburn hair around her face a halo of fire in the soft bedside light, her face aglow with love and wonder. Georgine bit her lower lip as Katie flashed her a brilliant smile.

"George," she said, her voice husky with joy. "Come meet Christopher Thomas." She moved her arms so Georgine could see the baby, a perfect, long-limbed child with a thatch of dark hair and a dimpled chin.

Sorrow rose inside her like a cresting wave. Breathing deeply, she rode with it, stepping forward to the foot of the bed, consciously releasing her tension as it broke and crashed. "He's beautiful, Katie," she said quietly, the break in her voice almost imperceptible.

She longed to stroke the downy hair, draw a finger across the dimpled chin. She didn't dare. She could do this for a little while, pretend for Katie's sake her heart wasn't breaking. But not if she touched him. If she touched him, all would be lost.

"Christopher, your Aunt Georgine," Katie said. The baby flailed an arm and yawned widely.

Relief flooded through Georgine when everybody laughed. They were focused on the baby, not on her. She *could* do this. No one would suspect how difficult it was for her to be here.

"That kid has more aunts than fingers and toes," someone quipped.

A floor nurse bustled past her into the room. "Everybody said hello? Let's give this baby a break," she said, reaching down for him. She smiled at Katie, who reluctantly let him go. "I'll bring him back for dinner in a couple of hours. Promise!"

There, Georgine told herself. *It'll be easier with the baby gone.*

It wasn't.

"I still remember the night you were born, Katie," Leigh Brannigan said. "After thirty-six hours of labor!"

And suddenly all the mothers in the room were off and running.

"Elizabeth couldn't wait! I had her on a gurney in the hallway...."

"The twins were over five pounds *each!*"

"He felt like such a miracle."

"Even the doctor thought she was going to be a boy."

"...in the middle of the worst snowstorm in twenty-five years!"

It got worse. Mary had cute stories about her grandchildren. Emily, her daughter, had the latest pictures of the girls. Toni wondered aloud if it wasn't time she and Clark had a baby. Mary's daughter-in-law Julie, twenty years old and pregnant, talked about the names she and Owen were considering for their child. Wynona, a pretty teenager, eagerly offered Katie her baby-sitting services, and Isabel wanted to know when Christopher would be old enough to play with. Even Wyn and Izzy had at least the prospect of motherhood still ahead.

Georgine alone had no baby pictures, no stories, and no hope ever to have them.

Retreating to a corner of the room, she watched silently as Katie opened gifts, the knot of tension in her belly growing into an aching void that threatened to swallow her from the inside out. Every tiny T-shirt, every rattle, every bag of diapers reminded her of what she didn't have. Would never have.

The new mother tore into the balloon-bright paper of Georgine's gift and held up the boldly striped PlayBabies sleeper. "George, this is so cute! Thank you!"

Forcing a smile, Georgine managed a wooden, "You're welcome," hoping no one would notice the strain in her voice.

She closed her eyes for a moment, rubbing her fingers in small circles at her temples, then rolling her neck to release the tension that had settled at its base.

If she hadn't been so busy at work this week, she might have thought to mentally prepare herself for this. Or if the shower had been at Emily's house as planned, instead of in the maternity ward of the hospital....

If, if, if. She could play that game forever. The fact was that no matter how things might have been different tonight, Katie and Emily had babies and she didn't. Julie was pregnant and she would never be. Clark and Toni could talk about having a baby, decide, make plans; she had no choice. Leigh and Mary were grandmothers. Izzy and Wyn had babies still to look forward to. Even Ruth—though she'd lost her daughter young, she'd had Sunny's bright spirit to light her life for eight sweet years.

With a swift glance around the room, Georgine slipped quietly out the door. She doubted anyone would notice she was gone.

But she hadn't counted on Mary Lewis.

Which was silly, she told herself through her tears half an hour later, sprawled across her bed while Mary made a pot of tea. Mary Lewis could always be counted on.

By the time the tea was done, George had stopped crying. Mary set her teacup on the nightstand next to the bed, then took a seat in the overstuffed chair in the corner, sipping at her own beverage without speaking.

"Thanks, friend." George sat up against the headboard of her bed, leaning against one pillow and wrapping her arms around another. She took a deep breath. "When Annie was born—" She slanted a look at Mary. "Was that two years ago?"

Mary nodded. Annie was her youngest grandchild, and the last birth in George's circle of friends.

"I thought I was finished with my grieving," Georgine said. "I was really happy for Beau and Emily, and I didn't feel as if

34

their joy took anything at all away from me. So—this blind-sided me today. My reaction to being in the maternity ward. Seeing Katie with little Chris so soon after the birth. Hearing all those baby stories."

"I'm sorry it's so hard, Georgine."

She nodded, grateful for Mary's words of simple under-standing. "Grief is—so unpredictable," she said. "You think you've got it licked, then *pow!* Suddenly it comes out of nowhere."

George lapsed into silence. Mary sat quietly, as if she knew George needed her presence more than her words.

There were other times sorrow had surprised her. Once at the symphony, twenty years after the death of the parents she barely remembered, Beethoven's "Moonlight Sonata" had reduced her to tears. Her aunt had told her later the haunting piece of music had been her mother's favorite.

The smell of hamburgers cooking on a grill could even now bring back an entire day with her Uncle Frank, happiness washing over her like the waves at Mission Viejo where they'd played, then sorrow pulling her back into its powerful under-tow.

And for a long time she hadn't eaten *moo shu,* a Chinese dish she'd always loved, because the sweet, salty *hoisin* sauce turned bitter when she put it in her mouth, as bitter as the night Hector told her over a meal of Chinese take-out he was leaving....

"I still remember a sermon Chappie preached years ago," George said, breaking the long silence. "I thought about it on the way home tonight." She released her pillow and picked up the teacup and saucer from her nightstand. "He talked about mourning. How mourning our losses opens us up to God's comfort and healing."

35

Mary nodded. "From his series on the Beatitudes. 'Happy are those who mourn, for they shall be comforted....'"

Another moment of silence. "Thanks for being God's comfort to me, Mary," George finally said. "Your friendship is such a gift."

"Yours as well, Georgine. I've seen your loving heart at work so many times in our little group. I wish—" Mary stopped. "Maybe God will work a miracle," she finished.

George knew what Mary wished for her. What George wished for herself: a child to love.

"Maybe I'll meet a man who has children he would share with me," she said. "That would be miracle enough."

"Do you want to meet a man?"

"Good question." She paused to reflect. "I'm thirty-nine years old, and I've been single almost fifteen years. To tell the truth—I'm not sure what I'd do with a man."

Suddenly, for no reason at all, they both began to sputter. And then to giggle like schoolgirls. And finally to laugh: big, hearty gasps of laughter that spilled tea over the edge of their cups. It felt wonderful, Georgine thought. To laugh after crying. To love after grief.

But when Mary had left and she was alone again, neither the tears nor the laughter had eased the ache in her heart.

Lord, be my comfort, she prayed. *As you have been before…*

Three

At first Bronson didn't recognize the voice on the other end of the line. He and Mary rarely communicated; when they did, it was by "snail mail," Hong Kong to Portland and back. While e-mail had helped him build a delightful friendship with his niece, it hadn't touched his relationship with his sister. As Isabel had confided to her uncle, "Mom just doesn't get computers. You know?"

Once he'd established it was Mary calling, he'd known the news would be bad. Why else would she call? "What's happened?" he asked, his heart in his throat.

"It's Aunt Liddy."

"She's gone?"

"No—not yet. But she's in the hospital. The doctors don't know how long her heart will last."

Her heart will last forever, Bronson wanted to say. *So many people have a part of it.* He kept the thought to himself. It wasn't that heart the doctors were talking about, of course.

"She wants to see you, Bronson. Is there any way?"

He didn't hesitate. "As soon as I can get there. Tell her I'm coming, Mary. Tell her to hold on."

Please, God, keep her alive. It felt odd, praying. He'd gotten out of the habit years ago.

He prayed continuously for the next three days as he made travel plans, cleared the work off his desk, and tried to get some sleep on the fourteen-hour flight from Hong Kong to San Francisco to Portland. *Keep her alive. Let me say good-bye....*

He didn't know why that seemed so important, saying good-bye to Aunt Liddy in person. He wanted to sit with her, hold her hand, prompt her to tell him once again the stories she had told him as a child, tales that had stirred his imagination, shaped the decisions he made later in life, directed him halfway around the world to work and live.

He wanted to believe he could infuse her with his energy; that the connection between them was so strong, his presence at her bedside could keep her from failing. He wanted to believe the stories she would tell him would keep her alive a little longer.

Be honest, Bronson, he told himself. *You want her to live long enough so that she can infuse you with her energy.*

Curiously for a man as independent and resourceful as he was, he wanted to ask her, "What now, Aunt Liddy? What shall I do? Where shall I go?" The child again, seeking guidance; the student seeking inspiration.

When he arrived in Portland, he drove straight from the airport to the hospital, blasting himself for having stayed away so long. He'd been back to the States twice in the last several years, once to accept an American Journalists Award for his series on Chinese student unrest before and after Tiananmen Square, once to speak at a human rights symposium. Both times he'd managed to squeeze in a visit to his parents, who'd "retired" to a senior community in Arizona, but he hadn't made the side trip to Oregon to see Aunt Liddy or Mary and her family for more than four years.

It shouldn't be so shocking, Liddy's dying; her body must be weary after all these years. But it *was* a shock. He hadn't seen it coming; he hadn't been around to see her physical decline. Because she didn't talk about her health in her letters, in Bronson's mind she stayed the same: strong, vital, active, curious, engaged, and engaging. Healthy spirit, healthy mind. A healthy body was presumed.

Mary met him in the waiting room. "She's asking for you," she said, her voice catching.

She was still alive.

Bronson opened his arms and pulled Mary close, their shared sorrow breaking down the barriers that time and distance and divergent lives had raised between them.

Aunt Liddy opened her eyes when he closed his fingers around hers. "Bronson. I've been waiting."

"I know you have, Aunt Liddy. I'm here now."

Her eyes searched his face. "You *see* me," he'd told her once. "In ways nobody else does." She'd been pleased, but Bronson hadn't been sure at the time that he liked anyone knowing him so well. Not even Aunt Liddy. Now…it would be good to feel that someone knew him, he thought.

"What do you see?" he asked.

"Still easy on the eyes," she said, and threw him a wink.

He laughed. "Aunt Liddy, you old flirt!"

She sobered. "Do you know what else I see?"

"What?"

"I see that you're adrift and lonely, son."

So she could still do it. See him. He felt tears forming, and didn't know if they were in response to her observation or the simple fact that she'd observed.

"You're leaving me," he said.

She shook her head, to let him know he didn't fool her, but didn't pursue the subject.

"I was only a week back from China when I delivered you," she said instead. "Wrestled you into the world kicking and screaming. Your mama was crying, and I was, too."

"Why did you cry, Aunt Liddy?"

"Because you weren't mine."

He squeezed her hand. "But I was. I've always been."

"You didn't look so different than a thousand thousand other babies I delivered," she went on as if she hadn't heard. "With your dark hair and your jaundice, you looked like my Chinese babies."

He wondered if she knew how many babies were dying in China now. Probably. She didn't miss much, and certainly not about her still beloved China.

She closed her eyes and lay still for a moment, breathing deeply.

"You gave all of us life, Aunt Liddy," he said gently. "But you gave me your spirit. Baptized me with those tears."

She opened her eyes and smiled, and he knew he'd said the right thing.

"I've left you all the journals, Bronson," she said.

What journals? He frowned the question.

"From the China years. No one else knows everything those journals know. I never knew what to do with them. You'll know."

He didn't answer, only nodded and stroked his thumb across the back of her hand, tenderly.

"I'm glad you're here," she said.

"I love you." He was hardly aware of the tears sliding down his cheeks.

"Don't be sad for me," she said. "I've lived long and well." She smiled one last time. "And I have a mansion waiting. Even grander than Xi Jia Lou."

Four

A unt Liddy had a gift for joy," Mary told Georgine, her voice pensive. "More than anyone I've ever met." The friends were having lunch at their favorite restaurant, Windows, overlooking the twin glass towers of Portland's convention center and not far from the Child's Play offices where Georgine worked.

"You mean that she was happy—or that she made other people happy?" George asked.

"Both." Mary paused. "No—neither," she reconsidered. "*Happy* isn't the right word. Joy is different."

George nodded. "Joy doesn't depend on circumstances."

Mary flashed her friend a smile. "That's it exactly. Know what music she asked for at the memorial service? Beethoven's 'Ode to Joy.' She said she wasn't interested in people crying for her when she'd lived a long, full life and she was going home to heaven. 'Save your tears for the little ones who never get a chance at life,' she told me."

George flipped back the linen on the bread basket in the center of the table and removed a warm roll. "From what you've told me about her, your aunt did more than just cry for those 'little ones.'"

"Yes. And more than just talk. Even after she retired from nursing, she put in hours as a volunteer with a nonprofit agency, teaching young mothers how to care for their infants and toddlers."

"And she never had children of her own?"

"She said that they all were her own," Mary said. "Every one she brought into the world. Every one she cared for. 'I bear them in my heart,' she told me."

Dangerous ground, Georgine thought as she felt a lump rise in her throat. She searched frantically for an appropriate response, but all she could think of was that Mary's aunt had lied—not to Mary, but to herself. The children she'd nursed were no more her own than the children George photographed were George's. How could they be?

Not that she blamed the woman for her self-deception.

She drizzled a little more blue cheese over her cobb salad and changed the subject. "Your Aunt Liddy's church, where the funeral's going to be—it's the one on the coast your father pastored for a while when you were a kid?"

"Yes. In Depoe Bay. Mom and Dad stayed at the church a long time after Bronson and I left home, but it's been thirty-five years since I lived out there. Thirty for Bronson."

"Bronson? As in your aunt's last name?"

Mary nodded. "Bronson is my mother's family name. It's a Southern thing—giving old family names to children. My grandparents were from Alabama." She sighed. "I could have been a Harper or a Lambert, instead of a plain old Mary."

George smiled. "Nothing 'plain' or 'old' about you," she said.

Mary lifted her fork, tipped it toward her friend, and said, "Bless you, my child! There's a good reason I keep you around!"

"Of course there is," George returned, smiling.

They ate in silence for a moment. Mary seemed lost in thought. "I haven't told you much about my brother, have I?" she finally said.

"Nothing, to be precise. How come?"

Mary moved the salad around on her plate, set her fork

down, then picked it up again. "I'm not sure," she said, glancing up at George, then out the window, then back to her meal.

George waited, puzzled by her friend's sudden restlessness.

"I guess because I don't know him very well," Mary said slowly. "He's been out of range for a long time, living overseas as a foreign correspondent for a newspaper."

"That sounds interesting. Where's he based?"

"Hong Kong. He covers China, Korea, Japan, Southeast Asia. For an L.A. daily, so I don't even read his work very often. He's had a couple of things picked up by *Reader's Digest*, though—I'll have to lend you some articles. He's a wonderful writer."

"He's younger than you are?"

"Five years."

"Wish I had a brother. I always wanted one." George's tone was wistful.

"Wish I was closer to the one I have," Mary said. She pushed her salad plate away. "I don't mean just in miles. Bron and Aunt Liddy were a lot closer than he and I have ever been. Aunt Liddy loved me, too, but there was something special between her and Bron." She folded the linen napkin on her lap and laid it on the table. "I really think she held off dying until he got here."

"Didn't you say she lived in China for a while?"

"Yes. I suppose that was part of their closeness. Anyway—I thought when he first came back—" Mary stopped, then started again without finishing her thought. "It's been nice having him here," she said. "Isabel adores him. And he's been a big help around the house with all the extra people here for the funeral."

"But?"

"I just thought we'd have more to say to each other." She sounded sad.

"Did his family come with him?" George asked after a moment.

Mary shook her head. "No family. Bronson's never married."

"What?" George's eyes widened. "You have an available brother and you've never told me about him?"

Mary slanted an unreadable look at her friend. "Don't even think about it, George. Bronson is single all right—but available? As in emotionally? I think not."

"I thought you didn't know him very well."

"My point exactly. *No* one does. He's so…*aloof.*"

Georgine felt a flicker of interest, something beyond the friendly curiosity she'd expressed in the conversation so far.

Aloof. It was the word Hector had used to describe her when he left. It was a way to cope that she understood. Staying aloof protected one from pain.

But kept other feelings at bay. Like joy. And love. George knew.

Who was Bronson Bailey, really? Why didn't anyone know?

"Did I tell you about Aunt Liddy's instructions for the reception after the memorial service?" Mary asked brightly.

Georgine was startled by the change of subject and tone. "I don't think so.…"

"She said she'd like to go to one last church potluck. And then she made me promise to ask the pastor's wife to make her favorite chocolate pecan pie!"

George laughed. "You make me wish I'd known her."

Once again Mary was pensive. "You'd have gotten along famously, George. I'm sorry you didn't have the chance."

Georgine hadn't been to a funeral since Uncle Frank's, thirty years before, and wouldn't be going to Lydia Bronson's except that Mary had asked her to help out at the reception. She'd met Mary's Aunt Liddy only once, and the funeral in Depoe Bay, where Lydia had spent most of the last half of her life, was a good three hours away.

Weekend traffic on Highway 18 to the coast was heavy. By the time she walked into the Depoe Bay Bible Church, the pews were overflowing. She found a place at the back of the church and resigned herself to standing.

There was music, and there was Scripture reading, and a few words about Lydia Bronson's commitment to her community and congregation from the young pastor of the church. But the service consisted for the most part of impromptu eulogies. George listened in fascination as person after person rose to share their experience of their "Aunt Liddy," the name everyone except her siblings seemed to have called her. At some point, whether in her role as sister, aunt, friend, nurse, midwife, educator, or community volunteer, Lydia seemed to have touched the lives of nearly everyone there.

The eldest in a family of twelve children, she had decided at age eleven she was going to be a missionary to China, a decision that had never wavered during the thirteen years it took her to get there, one of her brothers revealed.

Such certainty of purpose! George thought as a man stood and made his way to the front of the church.

He turned around. George stared.

It wasn't just that he was good looking, though he was that. Dressed in dark slacks and a textured gray sweater, he stood tall, fit, and trim. She guessed he was in his early forties, though he might have been closer to fifty; he looked like one of those men who got better with age. His short dark hair was lightly salted with gray. Lines fanned out from the corners of his eyes and furrows etched his brow, adding character more than age to his striking face.

Still, it wasn't his looks as much as the way he held himself, as if he unquestionably belonged in his body; the light in his eyes, as if he saw things no one else did; the energy that exuded from his pores…

Even when he stood still, the air around him almost crackled with energy. George caught her breath as she felt an answering energy rise inside her and resonate along her spine. Something she hadn't felt in a very long time.

He ran his fingers through his hair and cleared his throat. "She really *was* my Aunt Liddy," he said. "By blood—my mother's sister—and by spirit."

Georgine felt her pulse quicken. Could this be Mary's brother Bronson?

"Her influence on my life has been profound," the man continued. He paused, his hands gripping the sides of the podium, as if he needed something solid to hold on to.

"In childhood, she taught me a love for language, a love for adventure, and a love for China that have come to define my adult life. She gave me my first book and my first bicycle. She taught me my first words in a foreign tongue. She told me stories—spine-tingling tales about a fascinating land across the sea where I now live and work. Aunt Liddy planted the seeds in me all those years ago."

So he *was* Bronson Bailey.

George leaned against the wall, her arms crossed, and studied him, watching the changing expressions on his face. Listening as he talked, but more to the nuances and undertones than to the words themselves. Sorrow, affection, tenderness, respect, all woven together in his cloak of grief.

She didn't see the aloof stranger Mary had described her brother to be. He was more self-contained than aloof, she thought. Aloof implied detached, unemotional. Perhaps detachment was the face he presented to the world, his professional image. But that image was no more Bronson Bailey than a photo was a man. Or than her own professional image was Georgine Nichols. Behind his words about his aunt she sensed a passion and intensity that resonated with her own.

"Emotionally unavailable," Mary had said of him. But when was the last time her own emotions had been available to someone else? To a man?

Not since the early days with Hector.

She'd told herself she simply hadn't met a man since Hector that she was interested in. But had she given anyone since Hector a chance? To know her? To be known?

She jerked away from the wall, frowning as she straightened, rubbing her hands up and down her arms as a sudden chill shivered through her. This was crazy! What was wrong with her?

"My aunt lived her life by a Bible verse she made me memorize when I was only five," Bronson was saying when she focused once again on his words. "'Whatsoever thou doest, do it *wholeheartedly.*' A large word for a small boy. But she wanted me to know even then how life ought always to be lived. As if it mattered. Because, to her, it did."

As if it mattered? Georgine wondered as she watched Bronson return to his seat. Meaning that for him, life *didn't* matter? She couldn't believe that. Not with his intensity. Not with his passion.

There was a time life didn't matter to you, some inner voice reminded her.

A soft arpeggio on the piano startled her out of her musings. The pastor once again was leaning into the microphone. "Lydia Bronson brought excitement, energy, and joy to everything she

47

did," he said. "We could not honor her more than to find the same delight she did in living, to enter every experience with the same enthusiasm." And with a short prayer, the service was over.

Georgine quickly made her way downstairs to the church basement as the organist played the promised "Ode to Joy." Her mind was in a jumble. She didn't respond to men this way. She didn't want to. She'd given up on men. As she'd told Mary not more than a month ago, she wouldn't know what to do with a man if she had one....

He lives in Hong Kong, she calmed herself. *He'll be gone in a couple of days. You'd never heard of him until a few days ago, and you'll probably never hear about him again—unless you ask. He isn't going to disrupt your life—unless you let him.*

Five

Bronson leaned forward with his elbows on his knees, supporting his bowed head in his hands, as the chapel emptied out. The pastor's final words echoed in his mind: "We could not honor Lydia Bronson more than to find the same delight she did in living, to enter every experience with the same enthusiasm...."

Delight and enthusiasm. Gifts Aunt Liddy had given him once. Gifts he'd lost somewhere along the way. No wonder he felt lonely and disconnected—he was. Disconnected from himself. From the forces that once had driven him.

But how could he feel delight in the world he knew? A world where prisoners were left to rot in cells for the sins of their political beliefs? Where soldiers gunned down unarmed, peacefully assembled students? Where wanted pregnancies were forcefully ended, and unwanted babies were strangled or left by the side of the road to die? Where ideology or money or power was more important than human life?

How could he feel enthusiasm for a job that seemed to take him deeper and deeper into the heart of darkness—into the evil that resided in men's souls?

So what now, God? What shall I do? Where shall I go?

Ah. So he directed his questions to God this time—not to Aunt Liddy, who would not have been able to answer them even if Bronson had had the opportunity to ask before she died.

Would God answer him? In that still, small voice he'd heard

about so often growing up? He waited in the silence of the chapel. Expectantly. *Come on, God. Prove yourself to me.*

Why didn't God write messages on walls with his finger anymore? Speak from burning bushes? Send angels down ladders that stretched from heaven?

"Uncle Bron! There you are!"

He sat up, startled, as Isabel slipped into the pew beside him, grinning as if finding him was the biggest event of her day. Her blond hair was pulled back in a French braid, but several wisps had worked loose and floated around her face, framing her large blue eyes.

"That was a neat way to say good-bye to Great-aunt Liddy, wasn't it?" she said. "With all those stories and everything. She was really cool."

Bronson's heart felt suddenly lighter. "She was very cool," he agreed, giving Izzy a hug. "I hope people tell half the good stories they told about Aunt Liddy when I die."

"I already know what I'm gonna say at your funeral," Izzy said.

"Izzy!" he sputtered, trying not to laugh. "Don't do away with me yet!"

"Oh, you're just in middle age now, Uncle Bron, you'll live to a ripe old age."

His mouth opened but nothing came out.

"That's what Mom said about Great-aunt Liddy," Izzy explained. "That she lived to a ripe old age and prob'ly all her relatives will, too. But when you die, I'm gonna talk about how you helped me with my school reports and talked to my class about important stuff that's happening in the world."

"But I haven't talked to your class—"

"I already talked to my teacher about it," Izzy interrupted, "and she said, 'Sure, if you think he's up to it,' and I said, 'Uncle

Bron can pretty much do anything, so I think he can handle a class of sixth graders.'"

Laughing, Bronson held up a hand to stop her. "Whoa! Are you sure? A middle-aged man heading for the grave ought to be careful what he gets himself into."

She rolled her eyes. "Oh, Uncle Bron," she said, in the exact tone Bronson had heard Mary say, "Oh, Isabel…"

She jumped up and grabbed his hand. "Come downstairs. I saved you a slice of chocolate pecan pie. Mom says it was Great-aunt Liddy's favorite. Oh, and Grandpa's looking for you. I was s'posed to tell you."

His father probably wasn't the only person looking for him, Bronson thought. He'd recognized several faces in the crowd, kids he'd grown up with who, though still recognizable, looked very much the way Izzy had described him: in middle age.

Didn't that say it all, he thought wryly.

"You go ahead," he told his niece. "Protect that pie for me! I'll be down in a few more minutes, okay?"

"Well…" Izzy was reluctant to let go of him.

"How'd you like to show your old uncle around the zoo next week?" he cajoled.

She brightened. "Really? Can Danny come, too?"

"Danny can come, too. Now give me a couple more minutes alone, okay?"

"I'll save your pie," she promised, and zipped out of the pew and down the aisle.

He sat back, grinning, and stared absently at the lakeside scene painted behind the baptismal at the front of the church. A white dove flew in the painted sky.

All right, God, he said silently. *So you're speaking through twelve-year-olds these days. Next week it's Izzy's class and the zoo. After that—I guess I'll just have to keep my ears open.*

Just so you keep your heart open, too.

He looked around, startled, but the sanctuary was empty except for himself.

He really did need a vacation.

The feeling was confirmed when he reached the church basement and saw Pamela standing behind the coffeepot. He stopped and stared, his breath catching in confusion.

Then she looked up, met his gaze, and smiled, and he realized it wasn't Pamela after all. She had the same elegant, willowy grace, the same shapely figure beneath her black silk dress, the same wheat blond hair, pulled back in a sleek style that curved along her slender neck. But her smile exuded warmth in a way Pamela's had never done. And her eyes...

He walked across the room as if her eyes were pulling him toward her—warm brown eyes, eyes he knew for certain smiled even when her mouth did not. Deep, dark, fathomless eyes. Eyes a man could drown in.

She just stood there, looking at him across the table, a Mona Lisa smile touching the sweet corners of her mouth, and he couldn't look away.

"Do I—do I *know* you?" he finally said. The stammer was unlike him.

"No." She looked down, breaking the connection between them. He felt at once bereft and supremely relieved. When she lifted her head again, her face flushed, she didn't meet his eyes. "I'm sorry, I didn't mean to be staring. I—" She stopped. "Would you like a cup of coffee?"

And suddenly she was the gracious hostess, pouring coffee from a silver-plated pot into a gold-rimmed coffee cup, her hands steady as she handed it across the table, her smile polite.

Had he only imagined the soul-searing intimacy of that look across the room? He had felt as if they'd *seen* each other, the way he'd always felt Aunt Liddy saw him. Almost as if they'd recognized each other…inside. Where it mattered.

"I'm Bronson Bailey," he said as he accepted the cup and saucer.

"I know." And then, in answer to his startled expression, "I figured that out from what you said upstairs. I'm sorry for your loss. I can tell your aunt meant a great deal to you."

He nodded. "Thanks. You knew her well?"

"No." And again, because it was clear her answer startled him, she explained. "Mary asked me to help out today. Your sister."

Before he could respond, she was pouring coffee for someone else, smiling, making small talk. He felt a hand on his shoulder and turned to find his father with an old parishioner, and for the next hour he was catching up with barely remembered acquaintances from childhood.

When he went back for another cup of coffee, she was gone.

"Bron?" It was Mary. "You all right? You look lost."

He combed his fingers through his hair. "Yeah." He hesitated. "There was a woman here earlier.…" He indicated the coffeepot.

"My friend Georgine. She's gone home." Mary was frowning. "What about her?"

Why did he feel so uncomfortable? "Nothing. We talked for a few minutes. I didn't catch her name, wanted to meet her."

Mary was silent for a moment. "Bronson," she finally said, eyeing him with wariness, "I love that woman dearly. She is a treasure of treasures. If you hurt her, so help me, I'll—"

"Hey, lighten up," he protested. What invisible button had he managed to push now? He added, lightly, "I haven't the slightest tendency toward misogyny, Mary. Besides, I'm only going to be in Portland for a week."

"A lot can happen in a week," she said.

Bronson studied her expression. She wasn't kidding.

He looked away, resentful of her implication. What did his sister know about him? What did she know about his life? She still treated him like a kid, still tried to control what parts of his life she thought she could.

Let it go, he told himself. *It's Mary. Still the same, after all these years.*

Why shouldn't she think he was the same as well?

Six

_G_eorgine looked up from the fall catalog mock-up on the drafting table as Kim swung through the door to the office, clipboard in hand. "Everything ready for the shoot?" Georgine asked.

Kim pushed her shiny black hair behind one ear as she consulted the list on the clipboard. "Lights set up, props ready to go, outfits prepped, snacks in the fridge. Rosie's already in the studio, ready for hair and makeup. All we're waiting for is—"

She looked up at the sound of a knock on the door frame.

"Maya Murphy. And this must be her!"

A redhead in her forties and an Asian girl about four or five, her straight black hair cut in deep bangs, stood in the doorway. The redhead smiled. "We must be in the right place, then," she said. "This is Maya." She placed her hand on the little girl's shoulder. "I'm her mom, Colette."

"Hi! Great, Mrs. Murphy, Maya, we've been expecting you." George stepped forward and shook the woman's hand.

"Please, just Colette. I'm not married."

"Colette." Georgine nodded, automatically conjecturing. Maya clearly didn't have any of Colette Murphy's genes. Maybe she was adopted, like Kim was. She wondered if the Murphys had divorced. How sad, after having assumed joint responsibility for a child....

She introduced herself and Kim, then knelt in front of Maya. A sweet face, shiny hair, sparkling eyes, good bones. She would photograph well.

"Maya, my name's Georgine. I'm going to be taking a whole lot of pictures of you. All you have to do is try on some pretty new clothes and have some fun. How does that sound?"

Maya stared at Georgine solemnly, then groped for her mother's hand.

"It takes her a few minutes to warm up," Colette said, swinging her daughter's hand. "She'll be fine in front of the camera."

They rode the elevator to the basement studio together, George with a pair of cameras around her neck. Kim engaged Colette in conversation while George played a version of peek-aboo to coax a smile out of Maya. Once in the studio, the little girl sat patiently while Rosie applied light makeup to accentuate her features and reduce the shine on her skin.

After the first five minutes with Georgine, she acted as if they were old friends and the camera wasn't even there. As George clicked away, three rolls of film for each of half a dozen outfits, the little girl told her about her teacher and her teddy bear and her best friend Jason and her mom's job at the TV station. "Channel 5," she said importantly. "She makes up the news."

Laughter from Colette on the sidelines. "I *write* it up, Maya, I don't *make* it up!"

By the time they were finished, Georgine had posed her model in overalls and coveralls; jumpers teamed with tights and turtlenecks; oversized shirts with skinny leggings. She had shots of the little girl with schoolbooks, a lunch box, a paint-brush, and a basketball; Maya twirling around with her arms in the air, swooping toward the camera like a buzz bomber, touching her toes with a crazy grin on her upside-down face.

In a larger company, half a dozen people might have been involved in the shoot. As creative director for Child's Play,

George functioned both as catalog coordinator and art director, overseeing the production, establishing the "feel," and designing the layout for each catalog. She hired some of the studio photography out, especially the stills, but she put herself behind the camera for most of the studio work and when they shot on location.

Kim prepped the clothes before a shoot—steaming and ironing—and played the parts of photo stylist and photo assistant, making sure the clothes fit well on the models and handling the logistics of accessories, props, and lighting. She also made sure the small studio refrigerator was stocked with juice and snacks, important items to keep their pint-sized models happy and refreshed. With the help of Rosie, a hair stylist and makeup artist they hired by the hour, the two of them could handle almost anything.

"Now wasn't that fun?" George asked as she set her camera down three hours after she'd taken the first picture. It was a long shoot for a child, but with plenty of snack breaks in between, Maya had been a trooper.

"Yep!" she said. "Can I have some more crackers now?"

Georgine laughed. "Only if you put some peanut butter on one for me," she teased. She'd seen Maya take great pains spreading a cracker with peanut butter during an earlier break and offering it to her mother.

"Okay," she answered brightly. She fixed a cracker for Georgine and watched her eat it, giggling when her new friend dropped crumbs on the floor. George made a face at Maya, which made her giggle more.

"Do you have a little girl?" she asked.

"No, I'm sorry to say I don't."

"Well, you should get one," Maya told her, very sure of her opinion.

"If I could get one just like you, I would," George said, tweaking the child's nose.

Later, after Colette and Maya were gone, Kim said casually, "You know, I think Maya's right."

George hung her camera bag over her shoulder and followed her assistant out of the basement studio. "About what?" she asked, pretending she didn't know. Pretending she hadn't been thinking about it since Maya had made her pronouncement.

Kim punched the button to call the elevator. "About you getting a little girl. You're so great with kids, and I know you've wanted a baby. Haven't you ever thought about adopting?"

"Well, of course I have!" She stopped, surprised at her sharp tone.

She didn't talk to very many people about the details of her childlessness, but Kim was one person who knew most of the story. It was difficult to work as closely as the two of them had for the last three years without finding out about each other's personal lives. Although she hadn't said anything to Kim about Bronson Bailey...

Because there's nothing to say, she told herself firmly. "To tell the truth, it was my ex-husband who thought about adoption," she said to Kim, her tone milder. "I was too stubborn to give the idea a chance. I wanted my own baby and couldn't accept that it wasn't going to happen."

The elevator doors opened and she followed Kim, whose hands were full of the outfits Maya had modeled. George punched the button for the fourth floor.

"So I lost my opportunity," she said. "I'm not going to find a man who wants to adopt at this point. I mean, if a man my age doesn't already have kids, he probably doesn't want any."

"I don't mean you and a man," Kim said. "I mean *you.*"

Georgine felt her expression go blank. "What? You mean me, alone? Without a partner?"

"Sure. Like Colette."

"You mean—Maya never *had* a father?"

"While you were busy taking pictures, Colette told me about the adoption. She knew if she was going to raise a child, she had to do something—she couldn't wait around for a man anymore. So she applied for adoption. She's had Maya for four years."

The elevator lurched to a stop and the doors opened. Kim stepped out. "Lots of women are adopting as singles these days," she said. "George, you'd be such a great mom! You could do it."

George followed Kim down the hall to their office, shaking her head. "*Lots* of women are adopting as singles?" she asked skeptically, unlocking the office door and holding it open. "I've never heard of such a thing."

Kim dropped the pile of clothes on her desk.

"This is the honest truth, Georgine." She held up a hand as if making a solemn vow. "You know my mom and I do volunteer work for the agency my parents used when they adopted me from Korea...."

"Yes. Far East Adoptions, isn't it?"

Kim nodded. "In the last few years, especially since China opened its doors to international adoption, I swear a good 25 percent of the people mom and I have talked to in the pre-adoption classes have been single. In fact, Far East encourages adoption by single women."

"You're kidding!"

"Nope. Why don't you come to a workshop with me? Just to get some information?"

"Why didn't you ever tell me about this before?"

"I don't know. You're so busy with this job...."

"You're right. It's silly even to think about it. Who has time?"

They were both silent for several minutes. Georgine watched thoughtfully as Kim tagged the pile of clothes on her desk as PlayBacks. The catalog samples would be passed along to Hadley, who in addition to her mail-room responsibilities coordinated the company's buy-back program. She would add the samples to the stockpile of good-quality used clothing returned by customers for credit on new items. The used goods were periodically donated to children's charities around the world.

Kim looked up as she finished the last tag. "Well, you know what they say, George—if people stopped to think about how much time and money it takes to raise a child, no one would ever have a baby."

"That's not true, though. People *do* stop to think about it, and they have babies anyway."

"Right." Kim eyed her boss. "They must figure the rewards are worth the investment."

"But *alone!*"

Kim pulled a paper bag from a drawer and began to place the clothing samples in it. "You probably didn't know that single women who adopt represent the second most stable families in America," she said. "After two-parent homes."

George shook her head in wonder. "Kim, how come you know all this stuff at twenty-five?"

She grinned and raised her eyebrows. "A mom and dad who loved me and brought me up right. You could do that, George."

"Kim—I'm thirty-nine years old."

"I know how old you are." Kim rolled the top of the bag

over and set it on the floor next to her desk. "And it's not a problem, unless it's a problem for you. You have to be at least thirty-five before some countries will even consider you as an adoptive parent."

"Really! But, Kim—"

"Do you know where I'd be if James and Linda Horton hadn't adopted me?" Kim interrupted.

Georgine shook her head.

Kim quirked a grin in her direction. "Well, of course I don't know, either. But I do know where I *wouldn't* be. And wouldn't *you* be sorry!"

George laughed. "You're right. I'd be completely lost without you. Which reminds me..."

And they were off and running, talking about permissions, locations, whether or not they should hire a dresser for the shoot at Bybee Elementary.

She couldn't get excited until she knew more about this adoption idea, Georgine told herself as she locked up to go home. It was dangerous getting excited. Getting her hopes up.

But she couldn't help it. Maybe—just maybe—her dream of motherhood could still come true.

Seven

ronson hadn't planned to stay the entire week in Depoe Bay.

After the memorial service, he'd dropped by Aunt Liddy's house to locate the journals his aunt had mentioned right before she died, thinking he would take them back to Portland to browse through. He was curious, especially after her comment that he'd "know what to do with them."

He was surprised to find the notebooks, numbered and identified by year, filling two large cardboard boxes, and even more surprised to see they covered the entire eighteen years his aunt had spent in China, 1931 to 1949. Why hadn't she ever showed him these before?

From the moment he pulled out the first volume, flipped it open, and started to read his aunt's perfectly formed Palmer-method script, Bronson was hooked. The words fairly leaped off the page with the excitement and sense of wonder that had always been elements of Aunt Liddy's approach to life:

Finally! From the upper deck today I saw the emerald hills of China for the first time, rising from the mists like the forgotten lands of Eden. Unimaginably, indescribably beautiful! How many years I've dreamed of this day!

Izzy had come by her fondness for exclamation points honestly, Bronson thought with amusement. He sank into a corner of the worn sofa and continued to read his aunt's words, feeling almost as if he were trespassing.

She wrote about the other missionaries she was training with, about the colors and sounds and smells of the open-air markets, about the polite but cautious friendliness of the Chinese people, painting vivid word pictures with a few quick strokes.

She wrote about her intensive language studies at Nanking. Her instructor in Chinese history and culture was also the administrator of the language school, and clearly someone Lydia Bronson respected and admired. In fact, she almost sounded like a schoolgirl with a crush. A different picture than he'd ever had of his aunt.

Dr. Weldon Knight. Why was the name familiar? By the time Bronson discovered a letter inserted between the last two pages of the first notebook with Dr. Knight's signature scrawled across the bottom, the name had cropped up often enough he'd already written himself a note to find out. He knew he'd run across the name before.

When he looked up from the final page of that first journal, he was startled to realize he'd missed the sunset. He drove back to Portland, spent the following day with his parents before they flew out to Phoenix, and was on his way back to Depoe Bay Monday morning—much to Isabel's disappointment.

"I'll come back next weekend and we'll do the zoo, Izzy," he promised. "And I'll stay around long enough to speak to your class next week. Okay?"

He was enjoying his niece, but with reservations. Her energy and exclamation points had been easier to deal with over the Internet than they were in real life. She made him feel old.

"Cross your heart, hope to die?" Izzy asked him, her eyes beseeching.

"Cross my heart, hope to die," he answered, solemnly drawing an *X* over his heart with a finger.

The atmosphere between himself and Mary was more chilly. The closeness he'd felt to his sister in the hospital when he'd first arrived had slipped away. Their brief exchange about her friend Georgine had angered him at first, and then, he realized, hurt him.

Mary had already gone away to college when he first began dating in high school, and she hadn't lived near him since. Why would she think he'd treat women in any other way than with consideration and respect? He'd always been honest about what he was willing and unwilling to give, what he wanted and didn't want.

The problem was, he reflected during the three-hour drive back to the coast, that right now he didn't know *what* he wanted. Only that he didn't want what he had now: an empty apartment to come home to; acquaintances and business associates rather than friends; a job that made him soul weary and no longer filled the needs it once had.

Or maybe his needs had changed. Why else would he still feel so disturbed about his research on China's missing children? Why else would Pamela's engagement have hit him so hard? Why else had he responded so powerfully to his brief encounter with Georgine Nichols?

But once he picked up Aunt Liddy's second journal on his return to the beach house, his questions faded. Everything except the words before him disappeared, and he read almost nonstop for five full days.

The journals were fascinating: thoughtful, reflective, rich in detail. And tucked between the pages of each of the notebooks except the final two were equally fascinating letters from Weldon Knight, the dark, bold slashes of his penmanship a contrast to his aunt's even, rounded letters.

Bronson had discovered that his Aunt Liddy's Dr. Knight had grown up in China, the son of missionaries; attended university in the States to study Chinese history and culture; and later returned to open the language school in Nanking, which served business and political interests as well as missionaries in training.

At one point, for a period of almost two years from 1938 to 1940, Weldon Knight had served as an advisor to Madam Chiang Kai-shek, which was why his name had a familiar ring: Bronson had come across it while doing research for a feature on Madam Chiang's influence on modern Chinese history.

Aunt Liddy and Dr. Knight had carried on a lively written correspondence over a period of fifteen years. The letters weren't personal, exactly, though Bronson wondered if in his own way Dr. Knight had considered them so. He wrote as if Lydia had been...not a sweetheart, but certainly more than just a friend. A kindred spirit, someone with whom he could share his thoughts and insights, his successes and his disappointments. Someone who shared his passion for China and her people.

I fear that yesterday and tomorrow are on a nonstop collision course here, one of his early letters read. *Chinese civilization is the richest in history and culture the world has yet developed, yet it is so inflexible as to be utterly inadequate for this changing world....*

Prophetic words, thought Bronson. If only the Western world had had access to this intelligent and insightful correspondence! Even now the journals and letters had historical significance. Aunt Liddy had left him a gold mine.

After she'd completed language school, the mission board had assigned his aunt and two of her colleagues to establish an itinerant medical ministry in the countryside. During her years traveling from village to village, her journals grew with descriptions of births and deaths and, mostly, the lives in between.

Where Weldon Knight wrote with broad strokes about national and international political intrigue, Lydia Bronson filled in the details of daily life, painting word-pictures in her journals of an ancient culture being pulled kicking and screaming into an indifferent modern world. Her focus remained on her personal mission: how best she could express God's love to the people she served, how best she could nurture that love in her charges. Her great delight and her great compassion shone through every word.

The notebooks covering the years of war with Japan, a war the Americans had finally joined after Pearl Harbor, were especially fascinating to Bronson. These were the tales he remembered from his childhood, stories of his aunt's life "as close to the shifting battle lines as I dare," she wrote, "always within the sound of the big guns...."

Transferred to an orphanage in a small city swollen by the addition of thousands of "warphans" and other refugees, she once again shared her faith in word and deed: serving meals, offering medical care, teaching illiterate women to read the simplified thousand-character Chinese text. At one point, after the city fell to the Japanese in 1939, she even led one hundred of her charges eighty kilometers cross country from one city to another.

The fighting in China, as Bronson knew, had not ended with the end of World War II. Aunt Liddy wrote in late 1946, with great sadness evident in her words:

No matter that the Japanese have been defeated by the Allied forces and withdrawn from China. The war is not over here, it has only changed hands. With the enemy gone the Chinese have become their own enemy, Mao's Red Army and Chiang's Kuomintang turning their weapons on each other with a vigor renewed by their mutual hatred. There is nothing I can do except love those people God has given me to love....

There it was again. Her sense of mission unsullied even by the vagaries of war. How had she remained so strong?

In 1947, the letters from Dr. Knight stopped. Bronson leafed through the remaining journals to see if the correspondence might have picked up again at some later point but, discovering no more letters, went back to reading his aunt's words chronologically. It took him several more hours—and Aunt Liddy two years and her own forced evacuation to Formosa on the heels of Chiang Kai-shek—to discover why she'd never heard from him again.

The sad news finally came from an American businessman who located her in Taipei. Weldon Knight had been incarcerated by the Chinese Communists for a year in the same prison camp where the businessman had been held; he had been found guilty of having a radio transmitter in his possession. They had been chained hand and foot to other political prisoners at Changchun, her informant told her, forced to attend courses in Marxist indoctrination and subjected to hysterical accusations and long interrogations.

Weldon survived the brainwashing with his spirit intact, Aunt Liddy wrote, *but could not survive the fever and chills of the malaria that finally claimed his life.* The words were smeared, as if her tears had fallen as she wrote.

The irony of his death at the hands of the Communists was not lost on either Aunt Liddy or Bronson, as he read her response to the news:

By the time he resigned as Madam Chiang's advisor, Weldon had come to the conclusion that the Kuomintang had the social conscience of a cholera germ, she wrote. *Yet his death came because in his official capacity with Chiang's government during those two years, he had been 'an enemy of the people.' God knows Weldon was nobody's enemy—only the emissary of peace, the advocate of good.*

I mourn his death, but no more than I have mourned his absence in my life every day these last two years....

And no more than I mourn leaving my adopted land and the Chinese brothers and sisters who have labored with me for the gospel of Christ. Tomorrow I leave for a country that has become as foreign to me in my absence as China was eighteen years ago when my eyes first caught sight of her velvet green hills across the waters of the East China Sea.

What now, I wonder, will God have me to do?

Bronson closed the notebook with his aunt's final words still resonating. Throughout her eighteen years in China, he mused, she had understood her call to missions as a call to love and a call to serve. Throughout the rest of her life in this little town on the Oregon coast, with an ocean between her old life and her new, she had never understood that call any differently.

What have I done with my call to love and serve? he asked himself. *Who have I loved? Who have I served?*

Yourself.

The spontaneous answer was humbling. With the gifts God had given Lydia Bronson, she had had a part in changing history, one life at a time. Her healing hands had touched a thousand thousand bodies, her healing spirit a thousand thousand souls.

But she had gifts that I don't have, Bronson told himself. *And faith I've lost.*

But faith he knew, suddenly, he longed for.

Eight

hat a difference a week could make, Georgine thought as she crawled along the Coast Highway, her windshield wipers barely keeping up with the water blowing in sheets across the road.

Last Saturday had been all blue skies and sunshine. The forecast for this weekend was torrential rains, and they'd already begun. One never knew what to expect from the weather on the Oregon coast, which was one of the reasons she liked it so well.

Still, after a full week of work, if she'd had a choice she'd have opted for a clear night. The drive had been exhausting. She probably should unload her bags at the Inn at Otter Crest before she even thought about dinner, but she knew once she slipped out of her shoes and collapsed on the sofa in Clark and Toni's condo, she'd be lucky if she even made it to the bed in the other room.

So she could stop for groceries.

Or call out for pizza after she checked in.

Or go to a restaurant and let somebody wait on her.

Tough call, she thought wryly, and pulled into the parking lot of a restaurant at the north end of Depoe Bay without a second thought. She pulled up the hood of her raincoat, grabbed her bag, and made a run for the door through the downpour.

Toni had given her a rundown of the dinner possibilities near the condo. "Nice atmosphere and *great* food," she'd said about the Tidal Rave.

The nice atmosphere part was true, Georgine observed as

she slipped off her coat and hung it up. She hoped that meant the great food part would be true as well; suddenly she was ravenous.

The waiting area was painted with huge crashing waves that reached nearly to the ceiling, rendered with such realism she could almost feel the spray the artist had sponge painted in white and pale green where the breakers tumbled over themselves.

Past the patrons in the dining room, through windows spattered with rain, George could see the surf like lines of wild, ghost white horses galloping toward the shore. She'd come to love the rugged Oregon coastline, so different from the flat, crowded southern California beaches where she'd played as a child.

She didn't even mind there was a half hour wait for seating; it gave her time to freshen up, and she had a magazine to read while she waited for her table.

Reaching into a side pocket of her handbag a few minutes later, she pulled out her reading glasses and a recent copy of *Reader's Digest*. As promised, Mary had lent her the magazine featuring an article written by her brother, reprinted from the L.A. newspaper he worked for.

She'd had it since before the funeral last weekend, but work had been crazy since she and Kim had started shooting for the fall catalog; she'd worked overtime every night this week.

Her finger tracked a path down the right side of the index on the cover of the magazine, stopping when it came to Bronson Bailey's name. Maybe it wasn't just overwork. Maybe she'd been avoiding the whole idea of Bronson Bailey....

Funny how last Saturday she thought she'd talked herself out of her interest in him in the time it took to walk from the back of the little church to the reception hall downstairs. And how one look across the room half an hour later had completely undone her. Forget simple interest—this was complex attraction.

She still didn't know what to make of the sensation of startled and inexplicable recognition she'd felt as their eyes had met. How was it that she felt she knew him? What was it that she felt she knew?

She opened the magazine to Bronson's article. "Gone Missing" was the intriguing headline. Intriguing, at least, until she realized the title referred to baby girls; then it was simply horrifying.

The Chinese authorities acknowledge one hundred thousand orphans in their country, he opened his article. *Twenty thousand are registered in state-run institutions. Eighty thousand are completely unaccounted for.*

Gone missing.

In the last twenty years, an estimated 15 million baby girls have disappeared from China without a trace.

Georgine read on, her heart growing heavy as she learned about China's struggles with overpopulation, the strictly enforced one-child policy, the traditional cultural bias against baby girls. Abortion and infanticide were endemic, especially in rural areas, and 98 percent of the victims were female.

But it was Bronson's story about a woman he called "Susan" that caught Georgine's heart.

With her own children and grandchildren far away, the wife of an American businessman in one of the richest provinces in China had offered to volunteer in a "child welfare institute" in her city.

The orphanage lay several floors up in the heart of a crumbling tenement building. The caretakers were mostly young women, in their early twenties if that; they spoke no English and Susan spoke no Chinese, so she never learned their stories. They kept the facility reasonably clean, considering the condition of the building, and fed the babies on a regular schedule. But they never picked them up, held them, talked to them.

In fact, the children got virtually no mental or physical stimulation except what Susan gave them. Infants wrapped in swaddling clothes so tight they couldn't move their limbs lay in cribs staring at the ceiling all day long; toddlers sat for hours in a courtyard with their arms and legs tied to bamboo potty chairs with plastic buckets set beneath to catch their waste....

Georgine lifted a hand to massage the bunched muscles of her shoulders. This was not the light reading she'd planned to do this weekend.

But she couldn't put the story down.

Susan hadn't planned on falling in love. But one tiny girl, delightfully responsive to her cuddling and cooing, had stolen her heart. *Mei-ming,* the caretakers called her. "No-name." But Susan called her Peanut.

Then one day as she made her rounds, Susan found another child in Peanut's bed. Puzzled, she asked the attendants through a series of gestures and hand signals what had happened to Mei-ming. Had someone adopted her? They looked at her blankly and shrugged their shoulders.

She left the orphanage deeply troubled. The next week Peanut was still missing. And others, too, she realized. When she returned the third week, she brought a translator with her.

That was when Susan found out about the "dying rooms."

After a short conversation with the translator, an attendant led them to a darkened room a floor above the nursery. Peanut lay in the corner under a pile of crumpled bed clothes, fighting for each breath. Her eyes drained yellow mucus and her lips were parched.

The caretaker dispassionately explained that the children in this room were ill. Without medicine, they would not get better.

The orphanage had no medicine.

So here they were, hidden away until they died. No use to care for them or feed them; that would be a waste of precious resources....

Susan had sought out Bronson, telling her story with the understanding he would not use her real name or the name of the specific orphanage. She was afraid of being barred from the institution, and by now the children there had become her mission. She wanted to urge others to volunteer, to send medicine and supplies, to pray.

A few orphanages in China are model institutions, Bronson finished his article, *where the children are happy, healthy, and loved. But too many facilities, like the one where Susan volunteers, are underfunded and understaffed by workers who have no training in child development or infant care. Even with a hundred Susans, they would not be prepared for the relentless flood of babies abandoned across China every day.*

A flood of babies abandoned every day! And here she sat, Georgine thought, wanting a child and having none.

"Georgine? Is that you?"

Startled, George looked up over her reading glasses to find Bronson Bailey smiling down at her.

"Oh!" She pulled her glasses off, confused by his sudden appearance just at the moment she'd finished the article he'd penned. "H-hello, Bronson," she stammered.

"It is you!"

He sounded pleased, she noted as she met his eyes. Eyes she remembered well: thickly lashed, silver gray with a rim of darker gray around the outer edge of the iris. Magnetic.

She took a deep breath to regain her composure. "Some

trick," she said, holding up the magazine. "Showing up while I'm reading one of your articles. How'd you do that?" She wondered if her voice sounded as shaky as she felt.

He laughed. "I can tell you for sure it's not psychic ability," he said. "I'm very surprised to see you."

The hostess interrupted. "Miss Nichols, your table is ready."

"Oh! Thank you." She glanced over Bronson's shoulder. "You're alone? Would you—would you like to join me for dinner?"

He looked surprised.

"Unless you wanted to be alone…"

"No, no. I'd be delighted," he said.

Minutes later they were seated across from each other at a table by the window, Bronson explaining he'd been sorting through things at his aunt's house all week and Georgine explaining that friends had offered the weekend use of their condo at a nearby resort.

"It's been a crazy week," she said, "and if I'd stayed in town, I'd probably have ended up working the weekend, too. I'm here for my sanity. No work, not even any professional journals. I brought the *Reader's Digest* Mary lent me, a couple of women's magazines, a video or two, and my walking shoes."

He raised his eyebrows and grinned. "Your umbrella, too, I hope."

It was nice to know he had a lighter side, Georgine thought. Based on her first encounter with him and the article she'd just read, she never would have guessed.

"A hood, at least," she said, feeling more at ease. "Fortunately, I don't mind walking in the rain."

He looked pleased. "Ditto. I wish I could stay the weekend and walk the beach with you, but I promised I'd take Izzy and her friend Danny to the zoo in Portland tomorrow," he said.

"Two of my favorite kids! You'll have fun. And be utterly exhausted by the end of the day."

"I don't doubt that. Give me a prison riot any day!"

"You're kidding, aren't you?"

He laughed. "Hard to say. I have more experience with prison riots than I have with kids. To be honest, Izzy makes me a little nervous."

"And a prison riot doesn't?" she teased. "I love your nieces and nephews," she added. "And your great-nieces."

"So you know the whole gang?"

"Except for Zach and Abby. They'd moved away from home by the time I moved to Portland and your sister welcomed me into the Lewis family circle with open arms. Whenever I need a 'kid-fix,' I know where to go."

"A 'kid-fix'?" Bronson shook his head. "I can't imagine."

George laughed. "You'd be surprised. Too bad you've missed out on their growing up. Not that you don't lead a very exciting life," she hastened to add. "I love Asia—at least the parts I've seen."

"You've been there?" He sounded surprised.

"I'm a photographer. When I was freelancing, I'd get sent all over the world on shoots for glossy fashion magazines. I didn't get much time for sight-seeing, I'm afraid, but at least I got a taste. I know where I'd like to go back to when I have the time and the money."

"Where?"

A waiter approached the table for their order and they fumbled for their menus. "Two minutes," Georgine promised him. When he returned, they were ready.

She grinned as the waiter walked away. "Impressed? I can be pretty decisive about the little things."

"How about the big things?"

"Harder," she admitted. "What about you?"

"Harder the older I get," he said.

She nodded. "It's all that weighing of consequences the young don't give a rip about."

They smiled at each other, understanding.

"You're headed back to Hong Kong after the weekend?" she asked.

"Not just yet," he said, without further comment. "Now—back to my question: Where would you like to go back to when you have the time and money?"

"Oh…lots of places. The Great Wall. Mount Fuji. The Greek Islands. The Taj Mahal. Montmartre in Paris. Mazatlán."

"Quite a wish list. How about Hong Kong?"

She raised an eyebrow. "You inviting me?"

"Maybe."

Good grief, she thought. They were flirting! It had been so long, she figured she'd have forgotten how. "I haven't been. You recommend it?"

"Hong Kong's the most beautiful and exciting city I've ever known. And a good base for traveling all over Asia," he said, waggling his eyebrows.

Oh, why not, she decided. She was never going to see him again anyway. She leaned her elbows on the table and rested her chin on her hands. "Tell you what," she said, fluttering her eyelashes outrageously. "Throw in a VISA Gold card and I'm yours."

"Done."

"And I thought you took your time with big decisions," she said, arching an eyebrow.

"This one's safe. You wouldn't get very far with my VISA card. In fact, you'd probably be better off with your own."

"Oh, no. I don't use credit cards unless they're someone

78

else's." She fluttered her eyelashes again.

He laughed. "You're knockin' on the wrong door, babe," he drawled. "I think you must be lookin' for the sugar daddy next door."

Much to George's relief, the waiter interrupted with a basket of warm rolls. Things were beginning to feel a little out of control....

"Mmm," she said as she lifted the linen from the bread basket and the sharp smell of sourdough rose between them. She tore open a roll and spread it with butter. When she lifted it to her mouth she saw that Bronson was watching her.

Something in his eyes made her blush.

When was the last time *that* had happened?

Nine

The scallops Olympus, which Georgine proclaimed heavenly, were completely wasted on Bronson. He loved good food, and the scallops sautéed with garlic, red peppers, sun-dried tomatoes, Greek olives, and feta cheese had looked mouthwatering on the menu. But his dinner companion was so distracting he hardly tasted his meal.

He was charmed. Georgine was intelligent, articulate, and interested in everything. And not afraid to speak her mind. Absolutely her own person.

On top of everything else, she was a beautiful, gracious, very desirable woman, and great fun to flirt with.

Her delight in the world reminded him of his aunt, as did her earnest convictions about her place in it. "I believe God gives each of us special gifts," she told him. "And I think our job is to figure out what they are and find ways to use them to make the world a better place. Like the woman you interviewed for your article. Susan. What a gift for compassion she has!"

"But I'm not so sure she's doing the best thing for those kids," he told her.

"What do you mean?"

"You don't miss what you've never had. Maybe it's worse for kids like that to be held once a week than never at all."

"Oh, Bronson, you can't believe that!"

The truth was he didn't know what he believed.

When he didn't respond she added, "Sometimes when it's felt like no one cared, remembering the way someone loved me in the past was the only thing that got me through. I have to believe it matters, Bronson."

Life matters to her, he thought. *Like it mattered to Aunt Liddy. And then, I wish I'd been there to hold you, Georgine. When you felt like no one cared....*

He gave his head a quick shake, as if the movement could dislodge the unexpected image of Georgine in his arms. It didn't work.

"What?" she asked.

"Nothing. Maybe you're right." He looked out the rain-spattered window for a moment, trying to gather his scattered wits.

George was quiet. When he looked back she was watching him. *Those eyes!* he thought.

"So what did you think of the article?" he asked.

"Fishing for compliments?" she teased. Then, more serious, "It was an excellent piece, Bronson. Well-researched, well-written. And heartrending."

He nodded. "I haven't quite gotten over it myself."

"Something to add to my prayer list."

He looked out the window again. "I'm afraid it's going to take more than prayer."

She missed a beat, as if his comment had caught her by surprise.

"It's a good beginning."

"I don't mean to ridicule your faith," he said, meeting her eyes once more. "It's just that when you've seen the things I've seen..." He didn't elaborate.

"It must be hard."

He couldn't believe how good that felt, just to have someone acknowledge the difficulty of the job he did. "Yes." He took a deep breath. "Thank you."

Her smile felt like a benediction.

"I wish you could see Aunt Liddy's house," he said, seeing her in his mind leaning on the railing of the deck with the restless sea behind her, her wheat-colored hair loose and blowing about her face, her brown eyes smiling....

He caught himself. "She called it Xi Jia Lou. House of Evening Splendor. The garden's overgrown now—a classical Chinese garden she designed herself. But the sunset's still as beautiful."

"I'll have to get Mary to bring me out," George said.

"Maybe you'll let me."

She looked puzzled. "When did you say you were going home?"

Home? he thought. Suddenly Hong Kong felt as far from home as anyplace he could imagine.

"I didn't. I don't know yet." Then he told her about his aunt's journals and Dr. Knight's letters and a New York literary agent he knew who was going to be in Portland next week for a wedding. Georgine listened intently.

He loved the way she listened. With her whole body, with her eyes, with her insightful and interested questions. Another way she reminded him of his aunt.

"The letters and journals are a front-row seat to eighteen years of China's history, George. It's fascinating stuff."

"You sound very excited about this."

"Yeah." He ran his fingers through his hair. "I am."

"There's nothing quite like the anticipation of a new project, is there?" Her brown eyes sparkled. "Especially one your heart's involved in."

He stared at her. "Yes! That's it exactly." Suddenly he remembered Pamela's comment: *"You've got that journalistic objectivity down so pat you wouldn't know how to get your heart involved if you wanted to...."*

He remembered, too, his silent denial. *But I don't have it down pat,* he'd wanted to say. *And I do want to get my heart involved....*

He doubted Pamela would have understood, even if he'd been able to tell her. He didn't completely understand himself. It was so new—so uncomfortable—this getting his heart involved.

But apparently not new to Georgine Nichols. George understood.

"Mary's told me how close you and your aunt were, Bronson," she said now. "This project would be like the two of you writing a book together."

He stared again. How did she do that? Articulate things he hadn't even articulated himself? She was right. Working with the journals would feel like working with Aunt Liddy. Keeping her alive.

"I hadn't thought about it that way."

"How would you approach it? Edit the journals and letters and let them speak for themselves? Or use them for research and write your own book?"

"I'm not sure yet. I thought a good agent might be able to help me decide where to take it."

"With the Dr. Knight connection—" Her eyes glowed with mischief. "Maybe you could write a romance novel."

He stroked his chin, pretending to consider her suggestion. "You might just have an idea there...."

Once again he had her asking, "You're kidding. Aren't you?"

"It's an interesting idea," he said, still serious. Then he sighed theatrically. "But I'm an old bachelor. I'm afraid I haven't an ounce of credibility in the area of romance."

She laughed. "I don't think I'll touch that one."

"Coward."

"You got it. So if you find a publisher, will you quit your job?"

"Not unless I have to. I think I might be able to wrangle a sabbatical."

She hesitated. "And you'll stay here to write the book?"

"Can't think of a better place than Xi Jia Lou."

"So maybe you'll have a chance to show me around after all."

Count on it, he told her silently.

He realized at some point during dinner that George had been asking all the questions and he'd been doing most of the talking. Typical guy thing, he supposed, but not typical for a journalist. He'd barely learned anything about her history and personal life. How had she turned the tables on him without his even realizing it?

"I think I'm going to call you Curious George," he told her as they finished dinner with mugs of steaming coffee. Decaf for her, but with a three-hour drive still ahead tonight, Bronson drank regular.

"A rather mischievous monkey, if I remember right," George said. "I'm utterly astounded you'd compare us!"

He laughed. "It wasn't the mischief I was thinking about, though now that you mention it...." He left the sentence hanging. "You don't *look* much like a monkey, either."

"Not much, huh?" She gave him a dark look.

He laughed again. "Okay, okay. Not anywhere close. Anyway—back to the point—"

"Oh! There was one?"

He ignored her teasing. "Curiosity's a wonderful quality. I like the fact you're interested in so many things. You'd make a great interviewer. Ever thought about it?"

She shook her head. "But curiosity's important in my work,

too, you know. In any kind of creative work."

"Of course," he acknowledged. "You do fashion photography, you said?"

"Mostly, now. I started out doing weddings and still shoot one every once in a while. And I like doing portraits. Children especially."

"Ever done any news work?"

"I've sold photos to a couple of news magazines when I've been in the right place at the right time." She grinned. "And once a photo from a fashion shoot in Paris helped catch a thief unlucky enough to run in front of my camera carrying the loot."

She told him the story, then briefed him on her job at Child's Play. "I like what I'm doing, but sometimes it really is too much. I could make it easier on myself by hiring out all the photography and concentrating on the catalogs, but taking pictures is the part of my job I like best. So I just keep pluggin' away."

"What would you really like to do?"

"And you call *me* curious?" she needled him. "Is this the reporter coming out in you, or what?"

"Seriously," he coaxed.

"Umm...I'd love to do a travel book some day. Not landscapes. People. People at work and play. So I'd end up with sort of a portrait of an area's culture."

"Do China. I'll write the text."

"You've got everything all figured out, don't you?" she teased.

He shook his head. "I'm afraid I don't have much figured out at all."

His tone was light, but it was clear Georgine wasn't fooled. After a moment of silence she said quietly, "That's the best place to start, you know."

Her gentleness twisted in his heart like a knife. He met her eyes, not hiding from her, letting the silence hang between them as they looked at each other, letting the air grow heavy with tension.

"Georgine," he finally said, softly, his voice caressing her name. He reached across the table and took her hands between his own.

She didn't resist, didn't look away, continued to meet his gaze directly. He liked that. Loved the warmth of her eyes.

He stroked lightly across her knuckles with the pads of his fingers; her skin was cool and soft, her fingers long and elegant, strong and capable. An artist's hands.

"What do you want to do with this attraction?" he said.

He heard her breath catch in her throat. "Do?"

"We can pretend it doesn't exist and go our merry ways—which to me seems a waste," he said.

"Or?"

"Or we can spend some time together. Let our attraction play itself out however it will."

She closed her eyes just for a moment. Did he imagine the tremor in her fingers?

"I'm not any good at this, Bronson," she said when she opened her eyes again. "Really."

But her fingers moved to intertwine with his, slowly, deliberately, almost as if they acted apart from her intentions. Her thumb stroked his.

He drew his brows together. "I don't know what you mean."

Her gentle exploration stopped. She held onto him tightly for a moment, then let go, letting her hands drop to the table.

"Holding hands…"

He waited, wondering at her sudden withdrawal. Not just her hands. Her eyes. Her *self*.

"What?" he asked, as gentle as she'd been with him.

She hesitated, then raised her eyes to meet his gaze once again.

"What?" he said again.

"Holding hands...is lovely."

Her eyes glistened with unshed tears. She had not been touched the way he had touched her for a very long time, he realized with sudden insight. Why? She was so eminently touchable.

He hardly knew what to do with her. His instincts were to gather her into his arms and kiss her silly.

A few minutes later, as they said good-bye in the parking lot standing in the rain, he had his chance.

He wasn't sure what held him back.

Ten

When Georgine woke on Saturday morning, rain still pattered against the rooftop, its rhythm steady but lighter than last night's drumming beat. She looked drowsily at the clock: her usual waking-up time. Too early for a weekend away. Curling up on her side, she closed her eyes and snuggled into the blankets, letting her thoughts drift.

What would it be like to have a man in her life again?

Do you want to meet a man? she heard Mary ask her.

It didn't seem to matter whether she wanted to or not. Bronson Bailey had appeared out of nowhere. And he'd made it impossible to deny the attraction between them.

She'd been both disappointed and relieved when he'd let her go last night without attempting a kiss. She hadn't been thoroughly kissed by a man for such a long time....

It wouldn't have meant anything, of course; neither of them was looking for a relationship.

Still...

It certainly had been fun to let go of her usual reserve and flirt for a couple of hours. She couldn't remember the last time she'd felt so wholly feminine.

She was glad she hadn't found out till late in the conversation that he wasn't returning right away to Hong Kong; she'd never have felt as free with him if she'd thought she might see him again. He didn't know how right he'd been when he'd teasingly called her a coward.

Let their attraction play itself out? It already had, she told herself. For all intents and purposes, Depoe Bay was as far away from Portland as Hong Kong was. If he stayed at his aunt's house, she might run into him once in a while if he came into the city to visit Mary, but she could deal with that when the time came.

They'd been pleasant distractions for each other for a couple of hours, she decided. Nothing more.

Funny, though, how her tiredness had slipped away in his company last night. His energy was like a tonic.

Apparently, thinking about him had the same effect. She wasn't getting any more sleep this morning.

Yawning, she climbed out of bed and wrapped her silk robe around her, luxuriating in its feel against her skin. Soft and cool. She'd almost forgotten what it felt like, being aware of herself as a woman.

Was she being truthful with herself about not wanting a relationship? *Did* she want to meet a man? Not a restless Bronson Bailey type who didn't want to settle down, of course. But someone who might be interested in family life, a man with children of his own, or even grandchildren...

Maybe it was time to dream again.

She thought about her conversation with Kim. If it came right down to it—if she had the choice—would she rather have a child or a man? She'd always thought about family in terms of both.

Which she supposed was why she'd given up on either. She wouldn't want a man who didn't want children. And a man who wanted children wouldn't want her. The possibility of having a child and not a man had never even occurred to her.

At her gentle tug, the drapes over the sliding glass doors leading to the deck slid smoothly to the walls on either side. The Inn at Otter Crest was built up a steep hillside so that every unit overlooked the ocean, and the view from Clark and Toni's condo at the top of the hill was spectacular, whatever the weather.

Far below, over rooftops and treetops, the gray-green waves snaked toward shore, breaking white around the jagged rocks that rose from the water's edge like fairy castles.

She curled up on the sofa in front of the window with one arm stretched across its back, sipping hot cocoa and listening to Debussy on the CD player. A wind sock on a neighboring deck caught her eye, twirling red and purple and yellow in the breeze. A bluejay hopped across the deck and a pair of squirrels chased each other in and out of the long-needled branches of a swaying pine.

When her mug was empty, she made herself a second cup, resettled on the sofa, and reached for the women's magazines she'd deposited on the coffee table when she'd unpacked. What a rare treat, she thought, lounging around in her robe and pajamas with no agenda. She felt absolutely decadent.

Opening the latest issue of *McCall's*, George went straight for the fashion feature. After more than a dozen years in the industry, checking out the work of other photographers and art directors was an ingrained habit.

Very nice, she thought as she surveyed the ethnic-inspired outfits in settings depicting five far-flung locales. They'd likely been filmed in one spot much closer to home, maybe even in a studio. Shooting on location was expensive.

She studied a particularly appealing shot, golden with warm afternoon light. *It might be fun to do some of those school-yard shots for the fall catalog in the late afternoon*, she thought. Kids playing with their shadows, or making shadow-pictures on a wall....

She shook her head. Why was work so hard to turn off?

What else do you have to think about? came the unwelcome answer.

It was true. If she let it, her job could be all-consuming. Maybe a Bronson Bailey type would be good for her after all, just as a diversion.

As she riffled through the rest of the periodical, a flash of red caught her eye. She flipped back several pages to see what it was.

Her eyes widened in surprise at the photograph. Babies!

A gallery of babies, lined up across the page on a red blanket with panels of red silk brocade hanging behind them. "Made in China, Loved in America," the white headline read.

She stared at the picture, seven babies sitting next to each other, all dark-haired, golden-skinned, and almond-eyed. Seven beautiful little girls.

Excitement began to build in her as she read about the eleven men and women who'd gone through their adoption process together, from the first preadoption meeting to their trip to China when they picked up their babies almost a year later. Out of seven adoptions, three of the new parents were single women!

There was a thirty-seven-year-old political activist, a Peace Corps alumnus. "You start out thinking you can change the world," she'd told the reporter. "And then you figure out *maybe* you can change a little part of it. I thought that's what I was going to do: change Kristyn's life. So what happened? *She* changed *my* life! And still is, every day."

Another woman, a university research assistant, was forty-six before she seriously began thinking about what she really wanted out of life. She realized she longed to be a mother. "I pretty much cleaned out my bank account to adopt Aimee," she admitted. "But I didn't think twice. She's worth every penny."

The third woman, like Georgine, had gone through unsuccessful fertility treatments earlier in her life. A pediatric nurse, at forty-two she'd decided to turn her bad luck into an abandoned baby's good fortune. "Since Tess has come into my life, my perspective has completely changed," she said. "Now I think of my infertility as lucky. If I'd had my own child, I wouldn't have Tess. I can't imagine life without her."

Lucky to be infertile. The comment was astounding to Georgine. How could she possibly think of herself as lucky?

She looked again at the little girl's picture and knew how. Tess was loved and cherished as much as if she'd been this mother's child by birth. Aimee's mother had said her baby was worth every penny. For Tess's mother, her child was worth every heartache she'd been through.

Georgine closed the magazine and stared out the window, barely registering the fact that the clouds were breaking up on the western horizon. Could it be only accident that this was the magazine she'd thrown in her cart her last trip to the grocery store? That Bronson's article about the plight of baby girls in China had found its way into her hands? That Maya Murphy had been her first model for the fall catalog? That Kim Horton, who knew adoption inside out, was her assistant?

Lord—am I going crazy, or are you trying to tell me something?

She showered and dressed in a warm turtleneck and jeans, absently, not realizing until later she'd put on one blue sock and one brown with her sneakers.

By the time she got back from town with a bag of groceries and fixed herself a sandwich and a bowl of soup for lunch, the wind had swept the rain clouds from the sky. A glorious day!

She filled her lungs with the clean, fresh air outside her door, zipped up her windbreaker, and headed for the tram at the end of the walkway. And as it carried her down the steep hillside to the rock-scattered beach below, it was a child and not a man Georgine dreamed about sharing her adventures with.

She imagined herself exploring the tide pools with an almond-eyed toddler, pointing out starfish, anemones, and urchins. The dark-haired child accompanied her, in her mind, on the walk to Otter Rock through the wet, fresh woods, where they stopped and held their breath to better hear the songbirds calling to each other.

Running her hand along the railing at the edge of Devil's Punchbowl, she visualized herself holding tightly to the little girl's hand—encouraging her curiosity, protecting her from danger.

A daughter would count these steps down the sea-cliff wall aloud with me, she thought as she descended to the beach south of Otter Rock. *She would pull me along this hard-packed sand in search of shells and pretty rocks, laughing and calling, "Mommy! Mommy!"*

And for once the echoing word brought hope instead of grief.

She climbed a barnacled rock and sat high above the beach, watching the activity below, then closing her eyes to visualize the scene with her daughter, who screamed with laughter at the gulls wheeling overhead, chased a golden retriever along the sand, clung tightly to the string of a bright red kite that swooped and shivered in the breeze.

The waves played background music as they swept over the sand, retreated, swept back again; rushing, restless, mesmerizing.

When Georgine opened her eyes and turned her head to gaze out over the sea, the western clouds were golden white, the sun a blaze of glory.

Eleven

Bronson was surprised how much he enjoyed his day at the zoo with Izzy and her friend Danny. He hadn't spent much time with kids, and though he'd enjoyed getting to know his niece through their e-mail communication, he hadn't been sure how their cyber-friendship would translate to real life.

Izzy reminded him of himself as a child, inquisitive, eager to learn, full of energy. If her mother wasn't careful, in a few short years she'd be jumping off cliffs and out of airplanes the way he had as a teenager.

Chasing after Izzy and Danny made him realize just how much older he was than the last time he'd visited Portland and the twins had been about the age his niece was now. He didn't remember feeling half as tired after a day with Alex and Eddie—and they'd been more than a handful. He couldn't imagine trying to keep up with a couple of lively kids on a daily basis. How did Mary keep up with them?

After dinner, during which Isabel regaled the family with tales of her zoo adventures, he retired to his room in the Lewis's rambling old Victorian for a fifteen-minute nap, then got out his laptop to check his e-mail and send an update to Stan in Los Angeles. Not that he had much to say yet, except that he needed another week or two to get his aunt's things in order before he returned to his job.

He didn't say what things; he didn't think Stan would be happy to know he was considering asking for a leave of absence to write a book. If he could get a publisher interested in Aunt Liddy's journals and Dr. Knight's letters, of course. And get a halfway decent advance to live off while he wrote.

Maybe settling down in Portland for a year was just the change he needed to get a handle on his life, figure out what to do about his sudden dissatisfaction with the status quo. He'd only been here a little over a week and already he was getting clues.

He smiled to himself at the notion that his unconventional way of life could even be called a "status quo." Maybe Stan was right, that if a man got too accustomed to bachelorhood and red Ferraris, a white picket fence and a family might seem exotic.

Nah, he told himself, twisting his mouth in a self-deprecating grin. But then he had a sudden image of Georgine at dinner the night before, her face golden in the candlelight, her chin resting on her knuckles as she listened to him go on about Aunt Liddy's journals, her head slightly cocked in a way that made him want to reach across the table and stroke the curve of her cheek. Her warm, brown eyes *seeing* him. Understanding.

"Careful, Bailey," he said aloud.

Of course, George's life hadn't been the most conventional, either, from the sounds of it. She was close to forty, unmarried with no children, clearly committed to her career. She'd traveled all over the world. Maybe meeting a woman like her, at this point in his life, was a sign, like Aunt Liddy's journals, pointing him in a new direction. There was no denying their mutual attraction.

A light tap sounded at his door. When he answered it, his sister stood in the hallway with a tray in her hands. A tantalizing aroma rose from the plate of fresh-baked cookies and a steaming mug of apple cider.

Make that two steaming mugs, he observed, lifting his eyebrows. This was more than just a food delivery.

"Okay if I come in?" Mary asked, sounding unsure of herself. Unusual for his sister, whom he remembered as never unsure of anything.

He followed her glance toward the laptop computer set up on the desk. "Oh! Are you working? I don't mean to interrupt," she apologized. "Would another time be better? I thought...we might talk."

With Aunt Liddy's death, a houseful of guests for the funeral, and Bronson's stay at the beach house last week, they hadn't spent more than a few minutes alone since he'd been here. Except for that brief, tension-filled exchange about Georgine, of course.

"I'm just getting ready to sign off," he said, stepping aside and swinging the door wider. "Come on in." Leaning over the desk, he exited the Internet, then pulled out the chair for her and took a seat on the edge of the bed.

"Those chocolate chip?" he asked, eyeing the plate of cookies.

"Just out of the oven. Izzy made them."

She set the cookies and one mug on a corner of the desk and carefully handed Bronson the other steaming mug, then sat in the chair he'd pulled out.

"After all that running around at the zoo today she had the energy to bake cookies?" Bronson shook his head. "Amazing."

Mary smiled. "She is. It was nice of you to take her and her friend to the zoo, by the way. Thank you."

"My pleasure," Bronson said, grinning. "That girl is something else!"

"I hope she let you get a word in edgewise."

"Once in a while. Of course when I could, I tried to impress her with my vast knowledge of zoology."

"And?"

"And she passed my words of wisdom on to one unsuspecting stranger after another—kid or grown-up, didn't seem to matter. And with such authority you'd have thought she was the junior zookeeper!"

"That's Izzy, all right. She gets it from her father, you understand."

Bronson hooted. "As if 'knowing it all' isn't a Bailey family trait!" he said. "I seem to remember you telling me a thing or two a time or two, big sister."

She looked sheepish. "And here I am forty years later, still trying."

He raised an eyebrow. "You're admitting this out loud?"

Mary nodded. "Hard to believe, I know! But I wanted to tell you I'm sorry about—well, the way I came across when you asked about my friend Georgine the other day."

Bronson met her gaze. "We haven't made the same choices for our lives, Mary. We're different people, with different values and priorities. But I don't think you were being fair to imply that my relationships with women are—" he searched for the right words—"less than honorable."

"You're right, I wasn't being fair. I don't know you very well after all these years. But I know how you were with Aunt Liddy. And I see how you are with Izzy. That tells me enough to know I overreacted. It's just that George is very special to me."

An uncomfortable silence followed, until Mary finally said, "So. Apology accepted?"

He eyed her roguishly. "Only if you give me the lowdown on Georgine."

"Bronson!"

"I had dinner with her last night," he added.

She looked at him with a blank expression, as if wondering

how such a thing could have happened without her knowing about it. "You did?"

"We ran into each other at a restaurant in Depoe Bay. She was in the waiting room reading a *Reader's Digest* article I'd written."

"She was?"

Bronson grinned. "I hate to say it, Mary, but you're sounding a bit obtuse."

"I am?" she asked, teasing now.

They both laughed, the tension between them dissolving. Bronson reached for another cookie.

"It's just so hard to imagine you met without my having engineered it," Mary mused. "So. Do you love her as much as I do?"

Bronson almost dropped his cookie. "You jump pretty quickly from discouraging my interest altogether to asking if I've fallen in love! It's a little early to tell after one impromptu date," he said wryly.

Mary's face reddened. "Well, of course, I didn't mean *that* kind of love," she protested.

"Of course you didn't." He lifted an eyebrow. "She's great, Mary. Pretty. Smart. Interesting. Has no annoying social habits, as far as I can tell. So what's the scoop? Why isn't a woman like Georgine Nichols spoken for? Or did she just forget to tell me?"

Mary sighed. "You're going to get me into trouble here. If she didn't tell you, maybe she doesn't want you to know."

"We didn't get around to it, is all," he coaxed. "I'm sure we would have if we'd had the time."

"I'm sure you would have. Charmer." She took a long drink of her cider, as if she needed the time to decide how much to tell him. "Okay. No, George isn't 'spoken for.' She was married once. Quite a while ago. They couldn't have children. *She* couldn't."

Mary gazed into her mug and added, almost as if to herself, "It seems so unfair. So many babies aborted or abused by their parents, and Georgine without a child...."

She looked up. "It caused problems between them. They've been divorced—I don't know—fifteen or so years."

He sipped at his hot cider, looking at his sister over the rim expectantly, then lowered the mug to his knee when she didn't continue. "You mean she hasn't found anyone else since then? Or doesn't she want to?"

"I'm not sure she knows the answer to that question herself," Mary said. She hesitated. "I've had seven kids, Bronson. I can't know how it feels to Georgine not to be able to have children. How it makes her feel about herself, I mean."

"How it makes her feel about herself?" Bronson asked, puzzled.

"Incomplete, maybe. Deficient."

"What? That's ridiculous! As if a woman's value depended on her ability to bear children!" He struggled to control his unexpected anger. "Mary, that's so—*third world*. This isn't China!"

She looked taken aback by his vehemence. "I'm not saying it's right," she protested. "But you have to understand, Bron..." She shook her head. "If you could see the way she is with children. How they respond to her."

She smiled. "When she first met George four years ago, Isabel pronounced within an hour that she was 'really cool for a grown-up.' The highest praise from an eight-year-old."

She was quiet again for a moment, then added, "Georgine wanted kids more than anything, Bron. So did her husband. To risk starting up a new relationship, falling in love, having to tell a man she couldn't have his children...I don't think she wants to go through that again."

"Not every man would see her infertility as a negative. I certainly don't."

Mary's expression was thoughtful. "True…" Then she shook her head. "It's not my place to say what Georgine feels and doesn't feel," she said, getting up. "I've said far more than I have a right to. Talk to Georgine."

He rose from the bed, picking up the tray and reaching for her mug before placing his own on it. "I'll wash these up," he said. Then, quietly, "You're not still afraid I'll hurt her?"

"She's a big girl." Mary studied him for a moment, pursing her lips. "And you—" She paused again, a smile playing at the corners of her mouth. For a moment she looked as young and mischievous as Izzy.

"I think you just might be a really nice guy. Even if you *are* my bratty little brother!"

Twelve

eorgine slumped into a corner of the sofa and stared out the window at the treetops. How could she feel so depressed when just the day before she'd been so exuberant? Nothing was different: the view was still spectacular, the sun was still shining, the waves were still rolling in to shore.

She glanced at the *McCall's* magazine tossed on the end table where she'd left it yesterday. The article that had set her dreams in delirious motion was still there. China was still across the ocean, and tens of thousands of baby girls still needed someone to love them....

So what!

Who was she trying to fool? What in the world had she been thinking? Adopting a baby? By herself?

She didn't know where her mind had been yesterday—off in the clouds somewhere, apparently. This morning, without even trying, she could think of half a dozen reasons why adoption would never work.

Why couldn't she just accept the fact that she was never meant to be a mother?

Feeling sorry for yourself, Georgine? a voice whispered inside her head.

I'm just being practical!

Practical or afraid?

Silence. She let her head drop and lifted a hand to massage the back of her neck.

"Okay," she mumbled. "I'm afraid. Happy now?"

No shame in being afraid, Georgine. Unless you let it control you....

Her Bible lay unopened on her lap. She'd meant to have her own Sunday morning church service, but she'd been sitting here for an hour, staring out the window. Now, turning to her favorite psalm, she read its words aloud, letting the lovely seventeenth-century English roll off her tongue, making it a prayer:

"O Lord, thou hast searched me and known me. Thou knowest my downsitting and mine uprising; thou understand-est my thought afar off...."

At the end of the chapter, her tone became almost urgent: "Search me, O God, and know my heart; try me, and know my thoughts.... Lead me in the way everlasting."

She spent the rest of the morning on the beach, hunched against a cold wind blowing off the ocean. Her hike along the shore was a much more somber affair than yesterday's adventure. She walked with her head down and her hands buried in the pockets of her jeans, wandering in her mind as her feet wandered down the sand, trying to identify her feelings.

Oh, for the days when she'd been happy just to deny them!

She kicked a stone ahead of her, caught up to it, and kicked it again.

Of course she hadn't really been happy. She hadn't been anything but driven.

Climbing the same rock she'd climbed the day before, she sat with her knees pulled up, listening to the mournful cry of the seagulls and remembering.

Life goes on, she'd lectured herself after Hector had packed up his belongings and gone. She'd dumped her messy feelings in a pit in her soul and covered them over with glib assurances: "I'm fine, really! I have so much to be thankful for!"

And then she'd thrown herself into school and work with

such energy and singleness of mind that within a few short years she'd become one of fashion's most sought-after photographers. She won awards. She had more work than she possibly could do. Her services demanded top dollar. By the time she was thirty, Georgine Nichols had the world by the tail.

It lasted till the day her buried grief erupted without warning, in the middle of a two-week shoot in Mexico. A child model reminded her too much of the son she and Hector might have had—if things had worked out differently.

She cried for a week. Couldn't stop. Thought she was going crazy. Another photographer had to finish the shoot.

She didn't pick up her camera again for almost a year. Wasn't interested. In anything. Didn't care.

At rock bottom, she'd finally poured out her pain—and in the light of God's love and grace found healing.

Since then, those words she'd read this morning had become her constant prayer: *Search me, O God, and know my heart; try me, and know my thoughts....*

It was better to know.

"What am I afraid of, God?" she murmured.

A lot, it turned out. Enough that she spent the rest of the day thinking about it.

Raising a child was expensive even for a couple, she told herself. Without a husband, money she was used to spending on antiques and manicures and new clothes would go to braces and piano lessons and a college fund instead.

Hah! Braces and piano lessons and a college fund? She was still dreaming. If she cut back her hours at work to take care of a child, her income wouldn't even be enough to pay the mortgage. If she continued to work full time, her money would go to child care. And if she left her daughter in child care all day, what, exactly, was the point of having a child?

How did single moms do it? Take care of their families and work to support them financially as well? Play the roles of mother and father both?

Yet she knew they did. And did it well. Felice, the designer at Child's Play, had a daughter she'd raised alone since Bianca was three. Her friend Toni, though she'd had to work through her addiction issues first, had done a terrific job with Danny before she'd remarried. Colette Murphy seemed to be doing fine with little Maya. And what about the single women in the magazine article who'd actually *chosen* to raise their adopted daughters alone?

Of course, Felice had had her parents' support. And Toni's dad had been a huge help with his grandson. And the adopting moms in the *McCall's* article had all talked about the importance of their strong support systems: moms and dads to be grandparents, brothers and sisters to be aunts and uncles.

Who did Georgine have? Who would be there to help her out if she got sick? Or had a deadline she could meet only if she stayed at work till midnight? Or if she simply needed a break from her responsibilities?

She was an only child. Her parents were gone. She rarely saw the aunt who'd raised her; Ione lived in Montana. Besides, her aunt had never had children of her own and had never related to George's desire for family. She'd even tried to talk her niece out of her marriage to Hector. "You have so much talent, Georgine! Surely you don't want to end up just a wife and mother?"

Of course her aunt's discouragement had only spurred George on. "Ending up just a wife and mother" had been exactly what she wanted.

The conversation inside her head continued as she made her way back to the condo, fixed herself a tuna salad for lunch, ate it on the chaise longue on the deck.

There was the nature/nurture question psychologists were still arguing over. Who knew for certain how a child with unknown genes might turn out, no matter how much love was lavished on her?

But then, who knew for certain how a child with a *known* genetic makeup might turn out? Children never came with guarantees.

Especially when they entered adolescence, George reminded herself, thinking of a teen or two she knew about who'd turned their families upside down. It was hard enough being a teenager— but a teenager raised outside her race and culture? Trying to establish her identity, trying to figure out how and where she fit into the scheme of things? How much could Georgine help her? How would they feel connected? How would they under- stand each other?

Maybe raising a daughter would cause as much heartache as her childlessness had caused. Maybe more. You could resign yourself to never having children, but how could you ever resign yourself to a child who hated you? Or worse, made dan- gerous choices for herself because she hated you?

But Kim and her mother made it through adolescence, she reminded herself. *Beautifully.*

She descended to the beach at Otter Crest again after lunch, this time taking the steps instead of the tram, taking them fast, hoping the physical exercise would give her mind a rest. But she couldn't stop the questions.

Even if she did figure out how to make the logistics work, or at least felt confident she could make them work when she needed to—even if she could be the best of all possible moms—

Didn't every child deserve two parents?

Isn't one loving parent better than none at all?

Back and forth. For every question a response—and another question. Why did she have so many questions!

Had she been wrong all these years? she wondered. That this was what she really wanted—motherhood?

Okay, Lord, she prayed as she tidied up the condo and packed her bags later in the afternoon. *You've helped me figure out my feelings. I'm pretty clear about my fears. And they don't feel a whole lot smaller than they did before I knew what they were.*

So was I wrong to think you might be leading me? Am I trying to take things into my own hands that you never meant me to?

How do I know?

Where do I go from here?

She arrived at work Monday morning feeling refreshed and surprisingly at peace. God would lead her. He always had. Every time she'd been willing to ask.

In the meantime, she had a catalog to get together.

A few minutes later she was sliding a loupe—a cup-shaped magnifier—over the roll of transparencies laid out across the light table in the editing room, moving from one shot to the next with increasing delight. Her instincts about Maya Murphy had been right; the camera loved her.

The three rolls anchored to the table at the moment were shots of Maya in a green plaid, eyelet-trimmed coverall of soft combed cotton. The fabric was the perfect color against her golden skin.

In several photos she balanced a stack of picture books on her head. One of that particular series had potential for more than a catalog shot, George thought. Maya's lips were pursed and her eyes rolled upward in a comical expression that captured the essence of her playful personality. If the photo went nowhere else, it would definitely go into George's portfolio.

She'd learned long ago that the secret to getting great pictures was taking plenty of shots. Film was much less expensive than having to do a shoot over again, and sometimes she was lucky to get a half dozen good pictures out of three rolls of film.

A hand thrust too deeply in a pocket could make a pair of pants look lumpy; shadows created by a certain tilt of the chin could hide the detail on a shirt collar; shoulders too relaxed or not relaxed enough could cause a dress to drape all wrong. Catching her active, restless child models in the natural poses she favored and still presenting the garments in the best possible light meant a good number of photos ended up in the wastebasket.

This time, though, she was going to have trouble weeding photos out. She'd marked a good third of the transparencies with her grease pencil. And she still had five more outfits to look through—fifteen rolls of film.

She moved the loupe back to her favorite picture in the group and stared at Maya's image. What a sweetheart! *If I could get one just like you, I would...* Isn't that what she'd told the little girl?

She picked up the phone. "Hey, Kim," she said when her assistant answered the intercom from their office down the hall. "Could you look up the Channel 5 phone number for me?"

A few minutes later she'd reached Colette Murphy's voice mail and left a message for her to call when she had a chance. Who better to give her some perspective on the realities of adopting as a single mom?

By lunchtime George could hardly see straight, but she'd

narrowed down her photo choices to three for each of the six outfits Maya had modeled. She wanted Kim's input before she made the final cuts.

And she wanted Kim's input about something else.

"You busy tonight?" she asked when her assistant joined her in the editing room after lunch.

"Mom and I are doing a session at Far East. Why?"

George felt her heart begin to beat faster. "I wanted to ask you some questions. But... What kind of session?"

"We're starting a new cycle of preadoption classes. Tonight's an introduction to the agency and an overview of the adoption process, and then Mom and I talk about our experience from both sides of adoption, the parents' and the child's."

Perfect, George thought. She tried to keep her voice casual. "Would it be okay if I tagged along?"

"George! Really?"

"I'm thinking about adoption," she said.

There. It was out. She'd told somebody. Somehow it made the possibility seem more real. "But I need more information," she hastened to add.

Kim clapped her hands together, her black eyes shining. "I'll get you whatever you need," she said. "Oh, George. I'm so excited!"

By the time she left the preadoption meeting later that evening, head swimming with information and armed with a thick packet of reading materials, George was excited, too.

Not that her fears had dissipated entirely. But hearing her concerns voiced by other people who'd acknowledged and addressed and overcome them helped George put them in perspective.

"Can you love a child not born of your blood?" Linda Horton had asked rhetorically. "Of course you can. In some ways it's even easier. You're not looking for yourself or for your spouse in an adopted child, as biological parents often do. You're looking instead for the essence of the child himself. You accept his or her 'otherness'—a requirement for truly loving another human being."

"Can a child really 'belong' to racially different parents?" was Kim's rhetorical question. "All I can say is I haven't always felt as if I 'belonged' in my school or my town or my country— but in my family, I've always belonged. More than some of my friends felt they belonged in their biological families. The thing is, 'belonging' isn't a matter solely of culture or race. It's a matter of love."

Yes, George learned, the adoption process took a good deal of time and energy and money. Yes, it was full of surprises and setbacks and frustrations. But others had gone before her. Others had already proved the obstacles weren't insurmountable.

This could happen, she told herself in wonder as she drove home through the night. This could really happen...if she wanted it enough.

Thirteen

It wasn't that Bronson didn't have plenty on his mind already. He had a week to get together a book proposal before his New York contact came to town. He'd promised Izzy he would speak to her class about current events in the Far East. Stan was badgering him about when he planned to return to work. And he was living out of a suitcase packed for a much shorter trip than this one had turned out to be.

But no matter where he was focused at any given time, Georgine was always there, at the edge of his mind. He heard her laughter, saw the teasing light in her brown eyes, felt her fingers wrapped around his own.

Imagined her kiss.

He called her Monday night to tell her how much he'd enjoyed their dinner together in Depoe Bay. She wasn't home, and he didn't leave a message.

On Tuesday, after his visit to Izzy's class, he reached her at Child's Play. She sounded surprised to hear from him.

"I had a good time, too," she said.

"So how about lunch this week?"

She wasn't available for lunch. Or dinner. Either she didn't want to see him, or the impression he had of her social life from his conversation with Mary was dead wrong.

"I'd like to see where you work," he tried.

"Really?" Surprise again.

"You're not the only one who's curious, George."

She laughed. An involuntary shiver went up his spine. He loved her laugh. Low and resonant. Easy.

"It would be fun to show you around," she said. "Let's see… How about Thursday afternoon? I'll need a coffee break by three or so."

At least he knew she wasn't avoiding him.

On Wednesday he got his hair cut and went shopping. Conservative slacks and shirt, crazy tie—a grinning Curious George. Unlike any tie he'd ever owned, but he couldn't resist.

On Thursday at a quarter to three he parked his rental car on a side street near the Child's Play offices, in a remodeled warehouse in the eastside industrial district along the Willamette River. He shared the elevator up with an energetic young woman in jeans and a T-shirt whose short brown curls bounced even when she was standing still. He was almost embarrassed by the frank appraisal in her eyes.

"Know where you're going, or could I show you?" she asked.

"I think I can figure it out."

"Okay." She grinned as she hopped off the elevator a floor below Georgine's office, which was at the top of the renovated warehouse. The directory downstairs had indicated Child's Play leased both the third and fourth floors of the building.

A minute later he raised his hand to knock at George's open office, just in time to hear a voice over the speaker phone: "Hunk alert! Check out the gorgeous guy on his way up the elevator."

His face reddened as George and a pretty Asian woman both looked up from their desks and saw him standing in the doorway, his hand still raised.

"He's here, Hadley," George said, her expression pained. "Listening to your every word over the speaker phone."

"Oops!" Then the dial tone.

George grinned and rose from her chair. "Well, you certainly made an impression on our shipping supervisor," she drawled.

"The girl on the elevator? But I'm old enough to be her father!"

"Oh, Hadley doesn't practice age discrimination. Any hunk'll catch her eye."

He laughed. "I suppose I should be flattered." Raising an eyebrow, he added, "I assume you agree with her assessment?"

"Fishing for compliments again?" she teased instead of answering. Then, "What do you think, Kim?"

They both looked at the dark-haired woman who sat behind her desk with an expression of bemusement on her face. She looked from George to Bronson and then back to George. "Love the tie," she finally said to Bronson. Then, to George, "Where've you been hiding him?"

"It's Mary who's been hiding him."

"Mary Lewis?"

"Yep. Her long-lost brother."

George introduced Kim as her assistant and briefly explained why Bronson was in Portland—though not why he was in her office, he observed. He had a feeling Kim was figuring that one out on her own. The question was whether or not Georgine was figuring it out.

"I'll be right with you, Bronson. Have a seat while I finish up some details here," George interrupted his musings.

He took the opportunity to look around her office. Light poured in through plate glass windows with a view of Portland's skyline across the river. George's desk supported a Macintosh computer with a large, high-resolution color screen. Next to it was a drafting table where she sat on a high stool. The phone sat on Kim's desk, along with a stack of file folders and an open notebook.

Book racks along one wall displayed colorful back issues of

Child's Play catalogs and several unfamiliar trade and fashion magazines: *Communication Arts, Print, Vogue Bambini.* Another wall was covered with poster-size prints he guessed were from past issues of the catalogs.

If these were George's photos, she was very good at what she did, he thought. In one print, an adorable African-American toddler in a bright jungle-print swimsuit held a hose over her head, her eyes closed and her face scrunched up in a look of absolute, unfettered delight. In another, a set of red-headed twins about five or six mugged for the camera, their arms entwined and each sporting a black hole in his grin where a tooth had once been.

"Some of my favorites," George said as her assistant left the office. "Kids make such great models, don't they?"

He remembered Mary's comment about how well children responded to Georgine. "Either that or you have the knack," he said. "What are you working on now?"

"I have a day or two left on the summer catalog. A few more pages to format." She gestured toward the computer. "And Kim and I started our shooting schedule for the fall catalog last week. On time, for once. We outsource production overseas, and we can't start till all the samples come in."

"Where overseas?"

"Your neck of the woods. China, Korea, Thailand. We use a couple of companies in Sri Lanka and Mexico, too." She slanted a look at him. "Does that bother you?"

"Depends."

She knew exactly what his concerns would be. "Marty and Marilu, the principals, are pretty careful about who they hire," she said. "They have stringent standards about labor practices, and they won't sign a contract until they've seen a factory with their own eyes."

He nodded. Other American companies weren't as conscientious. "And you said you were shooting for the fall catalog? Do you always work this far ahead?"

"About six months. By the time this catalog comes out in early August, the Christmas catalog will be well on its way, and we'll be starting initial work on the spring catalog for next year."

"You sell children's clothes exclusively?"

"We do a few Mommy and Me outfits, but for the most part, just kids' play clothes. Three lines for children from birth to pre-teen." She leafed through a current catalog and pointed out the PlayBabies, PlayLittles, and PlayKids lines—fashionable, high-end clothes that looked, if one could tell from a picture, sturdy and well-made as well.

He took the catalog from her and leafed through it for himself, impressed with its whimsy and elegance. "This is beautifully designed, George."

"Thanks." She sounded pleased. "Want to see a catalog in embryo form?" She pulled from a corner of the drafting table a sheaf of papers held together by a large paper clip. "These are called 'thumbnails.'"

Each catalog-sized page of the mock-up she handed him was filled with sketches, pasted-in photos, and blank lines indicating where copy and headlines would be placed. "Product development—that's Marilu—lets me know what we're selling, how she wants each product displayed, what sizes and colors she wants photographed. The management team has already decided on a theme, so with that and Marilu's input, I create this first draft, which guides me all the way through the process."

"So the catalogs are yours from beginning to end?"

"Mine and Kim's. I couldn't survive without her. I'm lucky to have someone as competent as she is working with me."

"She's lucky to have a boss who appreciates her."

"You bet I am!" Kim breezed back into the office with her hands wrapped around a mug of coffee and smiled at him. "I'll take my coffee break in here so I can catch the phone, George. Go ahead and show Bronson around."

"Thanks, I will."

A few minutes later, both of them with coffee mugs of their own in hand, George guided Bronson around the third and fourth floors of the stylishly updated warehouse, explaining a little about what went on in each office: market development, product development, clothing design, quality control, inventory control, shipping, print production.

She introduced him to Marty and Marilu, the entrepreneurs who'd started the company, and Felice, the principal designer. And she went out of her way to introduce him formally to Hadley, who didn't seem the least bit flustered about having been caught in the act of admiring him.

"Hadley administers our PlayBacks program as well as supervising all the catalog and product shipping," she said as the younger woman beamed.

"PlayBacks?"

He was impressed when she explained the company plan that provided good-quality clothing to children's charities. Child's Play seemed to be a company with real heart. And George fit right in.

"I've got to get back to work," she apologized. "And I haven't even had a chance to ask you how you're doing on your idea for your book."

"I'll walk you up to your office," he said, lightly touching her elbow. Her head swung around, her eyes wide and startled, like a deer's eyes caught in headlights.

He dropped his hand. "If—if that's all right," he added, his eyes skidding away from hers.

"Of course!" Georgine's response was quick.

She could reduce him to a stuttering schoolboy, Bronson thought. How did she do it?

With an effort, he focused on her comment about his work. "I've got some interest in the book," he said, starting up the stairway. "I faxed several pages of Aunt Liddy's notebooks and a couple of Weldon Knight's letters to the New York agent I told you about, and then we had a long chat on the phone. She liked the idea of editing the notebooks and letters to create a sort of dialogue between my aunt and Dr. Knight."

Georgine followed him up the stairs. "So you'd keep their voices." She sounded genuinely interested.

"Yes. The book is theirs, not mine. They were *there*, right in the middle of the fight for China's future."

"And they had opinions?"

"Oh, yes. Passionate opinions. Usually they agreed with each other, but often they disagreed with other Western observers about what was going on in China and how events and policies were affecting the country."

"Kindred spirits," George said as they reached the landing at the top of the fourth floor.

He nodded. "Yes. But not clones. Dr. Knight's political observations and Aunt Liddy's more personal ones complement each other nicely."

"There's no indication of a romance between them?"

"None. Neither of them ever married, though. I wonder, if the times had been different, or if Dr. Knight had lived, what more might have happened between them...."

They'd reached her office door. "See? You've got the soul of a romance writer," she teased. "Sure you don't want to reconsider your market?"

"Maybe. If you help me do the research for the romance part," he teased back, waggling his eyebrows.

He followed her into the office. Kim was staring at them with a bemused expression.

"So you've arranged your sabbatical?" George asked him, either ignoring or unaware of her assistant's bewilderment.

"Still haven't asked. If this agent decides to take me on, it could take a while to get a publisher to bite. I need to work in the meantime. I'll probably fly back to Hong Kong next week and wait it out there."

I'll miss you, he wanted her to say. *I hope you sell your idea soon and come back home....*

Home? He was going crazy. Absolutely, positively crazy.

"Did you say you'll be in Hong Kong next week?" Kim interrupted.

He looked at George's assistant in surprise. Her expression had changed to one of suppressed excitement.

"Yes..."

"I don't suppose you speak Chinese."

"As a matter of fact, I'm fluent in Cantonese and Mandarin both. Why?"

Kim clapped her hands gleefully. "I think you just might be the answer to our prayers!"

Now why hadn't George been the one to say that! "It's been a long time since anyone thought I was the answer to their prayers," he told Kim, his eyes twinkling. "Care to explain yourself?"

She quickly laid out her problem. The adoption agency she volunteered with was sending a group of adopting parents to China the following week to pick up their babies, but the interpreter who'd been scheduled to escort them was on her back in the hospital, ordered there by her doctor until her own baby was born. The agency had been scrambling to find a last-minute replacement.

"Give me a name and number," Bronson told Kim, interested. His mind had been whirring as she talked. What a great opportunity to research a follow-up article to his "Gone Missing" series—an article about the lucky ones. The ones who ended up with someone to love them.

It would be a happier ending to the series.

And certainly a happier ending for at least some of China's children.

Maybe a happier ending would help Bronson, once and for all, lay the troubling story to rest.

"I need to check on a couple of things, but I'll give your director a call as soon as I can," he promised Kim.

"Great!" Her pretty face glowed.

I'd like to see that look on Georgine's face, he thought as he said his good-byes. *Like every time she looks at me...*

"I'll call you, George."

She lifted an eyebrow. "Sounds as if you're going to be a busy guy, Bronson." Unexpectedly, she winked. "Don't make promises you can't keep."

"Don't worry your pretty little head about that," he said, his heart soaring. "I don't make promises I don't intend to keep. I'll call you."

Going back to Hong Kong, even for a month or two, was going to be hard, he told himself as he strode to his car. He didn't want to go that long without seeing her. Without hearing her voice.

Things were going to happen when he returned to Portland. Of that he was certain.

Fourteen

im watched the elevator doors close through the hallway windows and turned to her boss with unconcealed delight. "George, Hadley wasn't kidding—the man is gorgeous! And in three years, I have never seen you flirt that way."

"Flirt? Me?"

"Don't play Miss Innocent with me, Georgine Nichols. I thought I knew you, but I think you've been holding out on me."

I think I've been holding out on me, George thought, smiling to herself. If flirting meant being aware of herself as a woman and acknowledging her awareness of Bronson as a man, she couldn't very well argue with Kim. He'd definitely brought something out in her she'd let lie dormant for years. Something quite delightful.

"I hope it works out for him to fill in for your translator in China next week," she said to divert Kim's attention.

It didn't work. "You like him, don't you?" Kim said.

"What's not to like?" she answered, lightly. "But if you're thinking this is going anywhere further than what you just saw, think again. Mary's already warned me he's not the settling-down type."

"Maybe he just hasn't found the right one to settle down with." Then, quickly clarifying, *"Hadn't* found. Till now."

"Kim, you're dreaming."

But she was dreaming, too, George realized when Bronson called the next day and her heart tripped over itself.

"Hi!" she said. "Life slowed down any in the last twenty-four hours?"

He snorted. "Hardly. I met with the literary agent this morning—she's agreed to take me on, by the way—"

"Good for you! Congratulations."

"Thanks. So I'm booked for L.A. early Sunday morning to meet with my boss at the *Examiner*, see if I can arrange that little matter of the sabbatical. Then I'm off to Hong Kong Monday afternoon. I'll meet up with the group from Far East Adoptions at Kai Tak Airport on Thursday and travel with them for two weeks—"

"Two weeks?" she interrupted, surprised. That was a piece of information she hadn't picked up at Monday night's meeting. "It takes that long for the parents to pick up their babies?"

"There are a lot of hoops to jump through. Also, the agency thinks it's important for the adopting parents to get a sense of their child's native culture, so part of the adoption package is a tour of China. We're going to the Great Wall, among other sites." He hesitated, then added, "Wish you were coming along."

Was she only imagining the longing in his voice? This couldn't be the same Bronson Bailey that Mary had warned her was aloof and hard to know, she thought. This Bronson Bailey had the soul of a romantic.

Or was it all show? Was he the kind of man who let a woman get only so far into his heart and then held her at arm's length ever after?

Where could that lead, except to heartbreak?

Then again—how much could she trust her own rekindled sense of romance? How much of what she felt with Bronson was just the newness of it all, the pleasure of being interested after being uninterested for so long?

Maybe she was the kind of woman who let a man get only

so far into *her* heart and then held *him* at arm's length ever after....

"Unfortunately, it's going to be all work and no play for me next week," she said, her voice light as she deliberately brought the tone of the conversation back to neutral ground. "I have a catalog to shoot. So...after the trip you'll stay in Hong Kong?"

His response sounded as carefully neutral as hers. "Yes. I should be able to get three or four articles out of those two weeks in China. Stan's given me a preliminary okay on at least one idea. I'll have plenty of work to do while I wait to hear whether anyone's interested in Aunt Liddy's book."

It could be months before Bronson was back in the States, George thought, relief and disappointment playing tug-of-war in her heart.

"I'm glad you called to let me know," she said. "Good luck, and—"

"Hold on!" he interrupted. "I didn't call to say good-bye over the phone. I'd rather do that in person. I know you said you were busy tomorrow night, but I'd really like to take you out to dinner before I go. Your date isn't something you could get out of?"

She was tempted. But only for a moment. Tomorrow night she was having dinner with Colette and Maya Murphy in their Northeast Portland home. "No. But I have a few hours between my photo shoot tomorrow and my dinner engagement. A walk would be nice to help me wind down, if you're interested."

"I'd like that."

A walk should be safe enough, George told herself. "Do you know the Grotto off Northeast Sandy and 82nd?" One of her favorite places in the city, and close to where Colette and Maya lived.

"I'll find it," Bronson said. "Just tell me when."

~~~~~

For months afterward she would wonder why, on that particular Saturday afternoon in the middle of March, she had let down all her carefully guarded defenses and let Bronson in. Closer than arm's length. As close as she had let a man get since the early days with Hector.

Was it the influence of her surroundings? George loved the shady paths of the Grotto, winding through sixty-two acres of gardens and woods. She saw it as a place of strength and serenity, a place she went to gain perspective when life felt overwhelming. A place of retreat, restoration, and renewal. Was that the reason she'd invited Bronson there? Because she sensed his spirit needed refreshing?

He was waiting at the edge of the parking lot when she drove in, dressed in jeans and a fleece-lined suede jacket she recognized as one Mary had given her husband, Mark, at Christmas. The weather was cool, but clear.

He looked perfectly at home in Chappie's jacket, even though she recognized the style wouldn't be typical in Hong Kong's cosmopolitan streets and semitropical climate. He was an odd mix, she thought as she lifted her arm in a wave across the parking lot. Well-traveled, at home anywhere and everywhere, yet not really home no matter where he was. Restless to move on to the next challenge, the next project, the next story, wherever it might take him....

"George, it's good to see you. Thanks for making time."

His smile was welcoming.

"You're persistent. I figured it would take less time to take a walk than field your phone calls till I finally gave in," she said.

"Smart woman." That smile again. A very nice smile.

She led him first to the cave for which the Grotto had been

named, an alcove carved into the side of a towering basalt cliff. A replica of Michelangelo's *Pietà* sat above and behind the stone altar. The outdoor sanctuary, hidden away among tall evergreens just off a busy thoroughfare, was lush with ferns and mosses. Several shelves of prayer candles flickered as the ethereal sounds of a Gregorian chant sounded from speakers in the trees.

"You still haven't seen the best part," she whispered as he stood in silence before the altar. "Ready to move on?"

The flat acreage at the top of the cliffs was home to a secluded Servite monastery, she explained as an elevator took them up ten stories; the wooded garden setting had been dedicated to solitude, peace, and prayer.

A canopy of green and a burst of daffodils greeted them as they stepped from the elevator at the top of the cliff. The distant sounds of traffic below and planes overhead enhanced rather than detracted from the sense of solitude; the sounds were there, but very far away. Like the mundane details of George's life seemed when she was here.

She guided Bronson to the glass-and-granite meditation chapel perched on the edge of the cliff, its graceful lines reaching toward the heavens like a prayer. Inside, a floor-to-ceiling beveled-glass wall offered a spectacular panoramic view of the Columbia River Valley and the Cascade Range in the distance.

George didn't need to hear him say it to know Bronson felt the impact of the beauty around them. At first, as they walked the winding paths through the gardens, they didn't speak at all except to comment on the view—here a parade of red and purple tulips, there a leggy camellia just beginning to bud; a crystal clear stream bubbling joyfully over the rocks, catching the late afternoon sunlight and throwing it back into the air.

When they stopped in front of the bronze statue of St.

Francis of Assisi, a bird on one shoulder, sculpted hands out-stretched to a lamb on one side and a wolf on the other, George realized she and Bronson were holding hands. Not awkwardly, but as if they'd been holding hands for years. She couldn't remember when or where on their wandering stroll their fingers had entwined.

"This place is incredible, George," he said, his voice hushed. "It feels like eternity here—like time has no authority, I mean. My life is so crazy—work, travel, deadlines, constant interruptions and emergencies. But here...I don't know how to say it. It's almost as if I can't remember how the craziness feels."

She squeezed his hand and smiled into his eyes, knowing she didn't need to say a word to tell him she understood.

They completed the circuit of the gardens a few minutes later, their steps slowing as they approached the elevator. Bronson came to a complete halt. "I don't think I'm ready to jump back into the fray quite yet," he said, searching her eyes. He rubbed his thumb along the side of her hand in an apparently unconscious caress. "Have time to sit with me a while more?"

"I know just the place," she said, leading him to a bench around a corner in the path.

They settled next to each other, Georgine leaning against Bronson's arm as it lay across the back of the bench. His hand dropped to her shoulder, and she instinctively nestled closer. Again, the contact felt as natural as if they'd sat this way for years.

Maybe it was his touch that opened her heart to him. Or maybe it was simply that he asked to know her heart....

"So much about you feels familiar, George. But objectively—I don't know anything except what you do for a living."

She could have come up with a pat response, she supposed.

I love kids and dogs, the beach and the woods, Chopin and Rachmaninoff. My taste runs to moo shu and tabouli, aubergine and hunter green, Dickinson and Austen.... Instead she said, "Ask."

"All right." He paused, as if thinking where to start. Then, "Who are the people you've loved? The ones who've influenced you most?"

She knew why he asked. His Aunt Liddy was still fresh on his mind. Her death, but even more, her life. The ways she'd influenced him. The ways he was different because he'd loved her.

Not a question a pat answer could even begin to address.

Maybe it was the combination of elements, she told herself later—the serenity of the Grotto, the tenderness of Bronson's touch, the sincerity of his question. She opened her heart as if she had no reason to protect it.

She told him all she could remember of her parents was the way her father lifted her in the air and swung her around, the sound of his booming laugh, the tickle of his mustache when he kissed her good-night. The way her mother danced her about the house, her laughter like a tinkling bell; the sweet, clean smell of her skin as she rocked her baby girl to sleep at night, singing softly: *All the pretty little horses...*

"They died when I was four," she said. "In a head-on collision with a drunk driver."

"Oh, George." Bronson sounded pained. "I'm so sorry."

"I went to live with my mother's sister and her husband. Aunt Ione wasn't sure what to do with me, but Uncle Frank—" Georgine shook her head in wonder. "How he knew what I needed, I'll never know. I adored him. He was my mentor and my playmate, my champion and protector. Photography was his hobby, and I was never in his way, not when I tagged along on his jaunts with the camera, not in the darkroom where he explained exactly what he was doing long before I could possibly have understood what he was talking about; not later, when I asked him endless questions about lenses and filters and f-stops and exposures. That was after he bought me my first camera, when I was eight. He never said he loved me. He just did."

"He was your Aunt Liddy," Bronson said, softly.

George nodded. "Until a month before my thirteenth birthday. His heart gave out."

She heard him suck in his breath as his arm tightened around her. "What a horrible loss. You must have been devastated."

"I was so *lonely*. You can't imagine how lonely…"

"What about your aunt?"

"Aunt Ione worked full time and started back to school at thirty-nine. She didn't have enough energy to deal with her own grief, let alone mine."

"So how did you deal with yours?"

"The same way she did. Or didn't, I should say. I stayed too busy to think about it. I studied hard. Took pictures for the school newspaper and the annual. Started a baby-sitting business."

"Mary's told me how good you are with kids."

"Has she now?" George wondered what else Mary had told her brother. "I do love kids. And back then, they were a lot easier to relate to than other adolescents. In some ways, I guess, the families I worked for took the place of the family I didn't have."

She fell silent, lost for a moment in her memories.

Bronson cleared his throat. "Mary also told me you were married."

She pulled away from the back of the bench to face him. This time she asked the question aloud: "And just what else has Mary told you?"

"Oops!" Bronson had the good grace to look sheepish. "She warned me I was going to get her into trouble. She wouldn't tell me much, George. Honest. Said if I wanted to know about you, I'd have to ask you." He slanted a mischievous look at her. "Besides—do you mean to tell me *you* haven't asked my sister anything about *me?*"

She raised her eyebrows. "Hardly anything."

"Ah." As if that said it all.

"You'd be disappointed if I hadn't," she huffed.

He laughed. A gray squirrel stopped in the path in front of them, staring, then scuttled away and up a tree. Bronson pulled George close again and gave her a squeeze. "Got me," he said. "So are you going to tell me about your husband or not?"

What to say about Hector?

"He was my first love," she said, simply. *And my last,* she added to herself. Why had she never found a man to replace him? "We met my sophomore year in high school. He was an only child like I was, but he'd grown up in rural San Diego County with dozens of aunts and uncles and cousins 'close enough to scratch when he itched,' he used to tell me. He was great with kids, and he wanted a big family like I did. I thought I'd met my soul mate. I thought I'd never feel alone again."

They'd married right out of high school, George explained, Hector with a good job working for one of his uncles, herself settling in to make their small apartment a cozy nest for the family they planned to start immediately.

"But I didn't get pregnant. One year, two years, three, four. Finally we consulted a specialist. Another anxious year, and then at last a pregnancy. Four months down the road—a miscarriage. More tests, more treatments, a second pregnancy—another miscarriage."

She related the experience in a matter-of-fact tone. But there was nothing matter of fact about the way George felt about her childlessness, as Katie's shower last month had once again reminded her.

"It was horrible. And as hard for Hector as it was for me," she said, feeling suddenly sad for the way their marriage had ended.

"But Georgine—he left you because you couldn't have a baby?" Bronson sounded outraged. "As if your only value was your ability to bear a child? What about *you*? A beautiful woman, inside and out—I don't get it. I can't believe any man in his right mind would leave you!"

George was startled by his decidedly protective outburst. "Bronson—that's sweet of you to say. And it certainly would make me feel better to label Hector the villain in the piece and be forever done with him."

She shook her head. "But that's not the way things played out. Hector said it didn't matter, he loved me, we could still adopt....

"That wasn't good enough for me. I wanted my own baby. It wasn't even *our* baby anymore, do you understand? It was *mine*.

"Hector was a good man. He was my best friend as well as my husband. But I couldn't be either his wife *or* his friend. He needed comfort. He needed to comfort me. I didn't know how to get into his grief, or how to let him into mine."

Bronson took her hand and stroked it gently before he spoke. "Of course you didn't, Georgine." Her eyes teared in instantaneous response to the compassion in his voice. "All your life you'd had to deal with your losses alone. How could you possibly have known? Who was ever there to show you?"

Turning her head away so he wouldn't see the tear escaping down her cheek, she said, quietly, "No one. No one was ever there." She closed her eyes and took a deep, shuddering breath. "I'd married Hector thinking I'd never be alone again. In the end, alone was the only way I knew how to be. I left my husband long before he left me."

Bronson lifted a hand to her chin and turned her face toward him, his eyes concerned. He wiped the tears from her cheeks with his thumbs. "You're an honest woman," he said, cupping her face in his hands. "And very brave." He searched her eyes a moment longer. "What happened to Hector, George?"

She lifted his hands away from her face, suddenly shy under the intimacy of his gaze, and turned her head away. The trees were black against an orange and purple sky. Where had the afternoon gone?

"As far as I know, he's still in San Diego," she said. "Remarried. I've never met his wife, but I've heard she's very nice." She looked down at her lap where her fingers were tightly intertwined.

Bronson remained silent.

"I've heard she's…a wonderful mother to their children," she said at last.

Before she knew what was happening, Bronson had gathered her into his arms. She relaxed in his embrace, letting him hold her, grateful for the comfort of his touch. Accepting it without thought for the future. Now was enough.

"I have to go," she said, her voice muffled against his jacket.

"I wish you'd stay with me."

She sighed in contentment, then reluctantly pushed away from him. He let her go as reluctantly.

"Thank you, Bronson. For asking, and listening, and caring." She smiled. "And especially for holding me."

Neither of them spoke as they descended in the elevator

and made their way in the gathering dusk to the parking lot. He walked her to her car and pulled her into his arms again. She kept her head tucked under his chin, not wanting him to kiss her. She was going to have a hard enough time missing his arms around her.

"Thanks for making time for me, Georgine," he said as he released her. "I'm going to miss you."

I'm going to miss you, too, she thought. *But life goes on. Life goes on.*

Fifteen

Bronson wrote a long letter to Georgine during his flight to Hong Kong two days later, wishing he'd thought to pick up some stationery at the gift shop at LAX before he'd boarded. His yellow legal pad hardly seemed the medium of choice for a love letter.

A love letter, he repeated to himself in wonder. To a woman he'd never even kissed!

There was no getting around it; no other description fit the rambling tome, so unlike anything he'd ever written. A love letter even though the only place the word actually appeared was at its close. Writing it even there had been scary enough—he'd toyed with *Warmly, Fondly,* and even *Best Regards* before biting the bullet and scrawling "Love, Bronson" at the bottom of the page.

And how long had it been since he'd actually set pen to paper instead of tapping at the keyboard? Almost as long as it had been since he'd felt the way he felt about Georgine—which as far as he could remember was in tenth grade, when a cheerleader named Bobbi Jo had set his heart beating in triple time with her flirtatious smile, and with whom he'd shared his first real kiss, under the football bleachers at the high school in Depoe Bay.

They'd "gone steady" for a month before she decided Lyle McBride was cuter than he was—not to mention a year older and the proud owner of a '64 Mustang convertible. A blow to Bronson's pride, of course, but also something of a relief by then, as he'd discovered Bobbi Jo didn't have an adventurous bone in her body or an original thought in her brain. To think he'd considered giving up both hang gliding and debate club for her!

When Lyle found himself at the altar the following summer, a shotgun urging him down the aisle and Bobbi Jo already showing under her white lace gown, Bronson had thanked his lucky stars he'd escaped with nothing more than a bruised ego.

Ah, the follies of youth…

Then he remembered George had met her ex-husband as a high school sophomore. A better match than most, it seemed, even at their tender ages. Clearly their relationship had been a world apart from his and Bobbi Jo's, despite its tragic ending.

There was no comparison between Georgine and Bobbi Jo, of course. It was the *feeling*…

As if the sky were bluer, the grass greener, the air sweeter. As if his heart had wings and he couldn't keep his feet from dancing. As if his very happiness depended on her loving him…

Every old cliché that popped into his mind seemed made to order for the way he felt about Georgine. It was almost embarrassing.

All the same, he hadn't put any of that in his letter. At least, not in so many words. It was soon enough to dream, but not soon enough to say it. Of all the risky things he'd ever done, making that plunge felt most dangerous. As it was, some of the things he'd told her he'd never expressed to another living soul.

He smoothed the pages out to read through the letter one last time, his heart rate accelerating. Was he brave enough for this? Letting Georgine know him?

Do you trust her heart?

More than I've trusted anyone's. Except Aunt Liddy's.

He told her about his meeting with Stan, who'd agreed to his leave of absence pending negotiation of the details. A page about his newest ideas for the book. And then a page and a half about Aunt Liddy, about the quality of their relationship—and about the ways Georgine reminded him of her.

She was a woman who lived out her faith, he'd written. *Whose life exemplified those famous "fruits of the spirit" my father used to preach about: love, joy, peace, patience, kindness, goodness, faithfulness, gentleness, self-control. I didn't remember those without some prompting, by the way; something inspired me to leaf through the Gideon Bible in my hotel room last night, and that passage struck me as an accurate portrait of my aunt.*

He was surprised at the amount of space he'd devoted to his own spiritual journey, how over the last few years his once vital relationship with God had suffered: *We've become somewhat estranged....*

God seemed so far away from the tragedies and abuses he wrote about; his faith seemed irrelevant, unconnected to the world he knew. Until the last few weeks—since Aunt Liddy's memorial service, really. Since he'd seen how many people's lives she'd touched. And since the words written in her journals had opened his eyes to the ways God had been present to her even in her darkest hours.

Maybe I need to refocus, he'd written Georgine. *Pay attention to the points of light instead of the darkness....*

Then he'd written a direct response to their last conversation: his sorrow for the losses she'd experienced, his admiration for her strength of character—her bravery and self-honesty. How good it made him feel that she trusted him enough to share her heart with him.

In fact, it was her trust that had inspired the last page of the letter—the page that made him a little queasy as he read it now. The page that felt most dangerous because it made him most vulnerable.

I've never considered myself emotional, he'd written. *In fact, I've been accused a time or two of being out of touch with my feelings entirely. But lately my feelings have been difficult to ignore. The research I did for my "Gone Missing" series, the surprise engagement of a dear friend, and the death of Aunt Liddy—all within a period of a few months—affected me in unexpected ways. I've felt lonely, restless, disconnected...painfully aware of the fragility of life.*

Meeting you has affected me in unexpected ways as well, Georgine. I don't know how to explain it, but being with you makes me feel alive, connected, and full of hope again.

I hardly know what to do with all this "emotional information," so different from the objective data I usually deal with.

I've put my career before marriage and a family, and I've never regretted my decision—until the last few months. Maybe I was so out of touch with myself I didn't know what I was missing. I've always enjoyed my relationships with women, but here I am at forty-nine, still a bachelor. Maybe I never met the right woman. Just as likely, I was never the right man.

I asked you what you wanted to do about the attraction between us and you never gave me a clear answer. So I'm asking you again. I'll be back in Portland sometime in the next few months, and I know I want to spend more time with you. I'd planned to work on my book at Xi Jia Lou, but I could just as easily rent a room in the city so we could see each other more often. What do you think?

I feel a little foolish writing a letter like this. It isn't a thing I've ever done before. But I'm feeling ways I've never felt before.

I will be waiting anxiously to hear from you.

Love, Bronson.

He took a deep breath as he finished reading. That last page disclosed more of his emotional life than he'd probably ever shared with anyone. But for the promise of Georgine Nichols in his life, the risk seemed worth it.

He tapped his pen on the tablet, frowning, wanting to add one last assurance to let her know just how much the possibility of having her in his life meant to him.

P.S., he wrote. *To set one concern to immediate rest—I've never wanted kids, and I certainly won't start wanting them at forty-nine. Except for Izzy, I'm not even sure I like kids! To tell the truth, just the idea makes me tired. It doesn't matter a whit to me that you can't have children, George.*

He read the postscript through and added one last sentence: *Two can be a family.*

He carefully removed the pages from the tablet and folded them in thirds. Pulling his address book and an envelope from his briefcase, he inserted the pages, sealed the envelope, and printed her name and address across it. He'd mail the letter as soon as he got off the plane. Before he could change his mind.

I won't change my mind, he thought, sure of it.

He leaned his head against the headrest and closed his eyes, his hands resting on the envelope as if to bless its contents. *Lord,* he prayed, *Georgine deserves the very best. Right now I can't describe myself that way—but I want to be able to. I want to be deserving of her love.*

I haven't asked for anything for years—except these last few weeks, that you would let me see Aunt Liddy one last time. And that you would guide me. I can't help but think that you're the one who led me to Georgine.

Make me a good and faithful man. The kind of man who knows how to love a woman the way Georgine deserves to be loved...

It was the longest and most earnest prayer he'd offered in half a dozen years.

Sixteen

"Wash or dry?" Mary asked as she pulled a pair of aprons out of a kitchen drawer and handed one to George.

Georgine eyed the mountain of dirty dishes from the Lewis family Easter dinner, covering nearly every inch of counter space in the cheery kitchen. "I'd find that question life threatening if I didn't know you had other people lined up behind us," she said. "I'll wash. You know where to put the fancy silver."

"I know—it's awful of me to make my company do the dishes," Mary said, squeezing detergent into the sink and turning on the water. "But I haven't talked to you for an age, and I figured a kitchen full of dirty dishes is the one place we won't get interrupted."

George pulled on a pair of rubber gloves and deposited a handful of flatware into the foaming water. "It has been a while, hasn't it? I've been swamped at work—we did a week-long shoot at Bybee Elementary School last week, while the kids were out on spring break. Ten to twelve hour days, including yesterday." She sighed. "No question I'm going to crash tonight. I might even fall asleep on your living room sofa before I make it home."

"Forget the sofa, you can have the guest room. Now that Bronson's out of it." She lifted a handful of flatware out of the rinse water, slanting a look at Georgine. "Speaking of Bronson..."

George wasn't going to help her out. "Heard from him?" she asked, her expression innocent.

"'Snail mail,' as he calls it, takes a week to ten days from Hong Kong, so no. But he sent an e-mail message to Isabel before he left Hong Kong for China. I thought maybe he'd have e-mailed you."

"Computer literate I am. Internet literate I am not." George grinned. "I think your brother was stunned to find out."

"Oh, I think he's stunned, all right. And I don't mean because you don't use e-mail."

George scrubbed at the spatula in her grasp as if it needed her full concentration. Mary was fishing, and she wasn't at all sure what or how much she wanted to say. Her feelings about Bronson were so fresh and felt so fragile, she wanted to keep them to herself for a while, savor them, protect them.

But she was curious, too. "What makes you say that?" she asked, not looking at Mary.

"The way he looked when he got back from your walk on Saturday."

An involuntary smile lit George's face. "Then he didn't say anything?"

"Honey, he didn't have to say a word."

Georgine laughed aloud at Mary's wry tone of voice. "We had a good time," she admitted.

"Just a good time?"

"No, we threw ourselves into each other's arms and professed undying love."

Mary almost dropped the butcher knife she was drying.

"Mary! I'm kidding!"

"Georgine Nichols, if I'd lost my toe——"

"Sorry." But her grin was unrepentant. "Couldn't resist the bait." She eyed Mary thoughtfully. "As I recall, your initial advice on this whole Bronson business was, 'Don't even think about it, George.' Have you changed your tune?"

Mary considered the question. "I don't know. Our visit ended differently than it began. We actually had a couple of good, honest conversations. Bronson seemed...*warmer* than I remembered him, I guess. More open." She scooped the last serving spoon out of the rinse water. "Maybe I've been selling him short."

George nodded. "I have to tell you your description of him as 'aloof' doesn't seem to fit at all." She remembered her first impression of him, of the passion and tenderness beneath his professional facade. "Self-contained, maybe, but not aloof. In fact, he's been very responsive to me."

At Mary's sidelong glance she added reluctantly, "Okay, okay. I admit I've been doing a little dreaming...."

The truth was, if she hadn't had so much to occupy her mind at work the last week, she'd have been in a constant haze. As it was, Bronson was the last thing she thought about at night and the first thing she thought about in the morning.

She loved the way she felt about him. Loved the energy that arced between them. Their "chemistry." It was all-encompassing—emotional, intellectual, physical. She knew it even without having kissed him.

She remembered the way his intensity and passion had called to her when he walked to the front of the church at his aunt's memorial service; the frisson of awareness when their eyes had met and locked across the room when he'd come downstairs. The way they'd *seen* each other. "Do I *know* you?" he'd asked. Startled more than unsure.

No.

And yet, at some deep level, *yes.*

That's why it felt so natural holding hands when they walked, she thought. Sitting close when they talked. Yielding to each other's arms for comfort and care. All outward expressions of something they both felt inside.

"I wonder where Bronson is in his walk with God," Mary interrupted her musings.

The comment caught her off guard. "We haven't shared much about our spiritual experience," she admitted. "My impression is that he's...searching. Trying to find his way back to a place he's been before, but not sure how to get there."

She pulled the drain in the sink and peeled off her gloves as she continued. "When Bronson described your aunt's journals, he told me how envious he was of her faith. How strong it was, how unwavering. And he made a comment, later, about feeling as if he hadn't figured out much about life. The two thoughts seemed connected somehow."

Untying her apron, she draped it over the dish rack where Mary had placed hers, ready for the "second shift" dish crew.

"I like him, Mary. I'm not sure what to do with that—it's been so long since I've felt this way, I hardly know how to act." She hesitated, then added, "I am feeling as if I'm ready for something more in my life than work. I mean, I like what I do, but it's not enough."

Mary didn't say anything, but George knew what she was thinking: *Work has never been enough. You want a family.*

Typically, she hadn't told Mary about the steps she'd taken to look into adoption. Both their lives had been so hectic they hadn't had time for more than a phone call since Lydia Bronson's memorial service. But even if they had, George rarely shared plans with anyone until she'd already processed her thoughts and feelings and reached a definite decision in her own mind. Unlike Mary, who needed to talk out her process aloud before reaching a conclusion.

And if George had been unsure earlier about the idea of adopting as a single, she was even more unsure since acknowledging her attraction to Bronson. It couldn't be just coincidence, she argued with herself—the man who'd written so passionately about the plight of abandoned baby girls in China, the man who'd motivated her interest in adoption, suddenly becoming important in her life.

It couldn't be just coincidence—could it?

She couldn't stop herself from dreaming. Maybe she didn't have to choose between a husband and a child. Maybe God was bringing everything she'd always wanted together in one beautifully wrapped package. Laying it at her feet.

Why would God bring Bronson into her life this way otherwise? she asked herself. After a dozen years alone?

Maybe she didn't have to be alone. Maybe she wouldn't have to face the fears that crowded in at the thought of adopting as a single woman. Maybe she wouldn't have to raise a child alone....

She jumped as the kitchen door banged open and Izzy came barging into the room, waving an envelope and laughing like a maniac. Eddie was close on her heels.

"Give that back, you little brat!"

Mary grabbed her daughter with one hand and her son with the other, which appeared to upset Izzy not at all and infuriate her older brother.

"Eddie's got a girlfriend, Eddie's got a girlfriend," Izzy announced in a triumphant singsong.

"Mom! Make her give it back!"

George leaned against the counter with her arms crossed, looking on with admiration as Mary handled the sibling conflict with humor and aplomb.

She grinned. At least she and Bronson would know where to go for parenting advice.

Two days later she sat at her kitchen table with Bronson's letter in front of her, the last page on top, staring at his postscript as if it were written in Chinese, and sick with disappointment.

It was the most romantic letter she'd ever received. And she knew he'd meant his postscript in the sweetest way: *It doesn't matter a whit to me that you can't have children....*

But she and Bronson clearly did not know each other in the way she'd fantasized they did.

Not sure he even liked kids? How could that be, when she identified with him in so many other ways? How had they so completely failed to understand each other about something so fundamental? The value that most transparently defined her? She loved children; she'd lived her life finding ways to have them in her life. Not only could she not imagine her life without them—she didn't *want* to imagine her life without them.

So God hadn't brought Bronson into her life to make her dreams come true....

Thankfully the truth had come out now instead of somewhere down the road. Now, she was severely disappointed; much longer and she might have been severely hurt.

In fact, the letter couldn't have come at a better time. She'd taken the morning off, comp time for the extra hours she'd put in last week. After a good night's sleep and a rare morning walk, she felt invigorated, well rested, and capable of handling the disappointment she'd been delivered in the morning mail. Reading Bronson's postscript after an exhausting day on location like she'd had last week would have felt disastrous. She'd probably be in tears at this point. As it was, her eyes were a little misty.

Maybe Bronson was her test, she thought as she rode the elevator up to her office later in the day. A test of her commitment. Colette Murphy had given her some important things to think about when they'd talked, and commitment was a big one.

"When you're truly committed," Maya's mother had told her, "the fears and the problems sort themselves out. I was scared to death about adopting a baby, raising a child on my own. I still get scared sometimes. But I'm Maya's mom. I love her. When a problem comes up, I don't have any option but to work it out—I decided that when I decided to adopt her alone. I'm a great believer in commitment."

How committed was George to having a child in her life?

If I have to make a choice...

The elevator doors opened and she caught sight of Kim bent over her desk in their office. She took a deep breath as she finished her thought. *I'd rather have a child than a man.*

She knew it with sudden, dazzling clarity.

"I've decided," she announced to Kim as she strode into the office. She hugged herself and twirled around. "I'm going to adopt!"

"George!" Kim leaped up from her desk, her face aglow, and hugged her boss. "That's wonderful! Mom will be so pleased to hear—we've been praying for you. That you'd know for sure."

"I know for sure. I don't know how yet, but—Kim, God has a baby for me. Some little girl who needs a mom as much as I need a daughter." She threw her arms out, happiness bubbling up inside her. "God has a child for me!"

For just an instant all her fears pressed in.

Are you committed to having a child in your life? she whispered to her heart.

I am, her heart sang in reply.

Georgine's fears slunk away in the face of her certainty. She was going to be a mother.

Seventeen

he letter from Georgine came a week after Bronson's return to Hong Kong from escorting a group of nine families through the final phase of their adoption process. He ripped into it eagerly.

Dear Bronson,

There is so much about your letter that tugs at my heart. And so much about you that I'm drawn to and admire. Thanks for writing about your Aunt Liddy. I know you were answering the question you asked me the last time we talked—"Who are the people you've loved? The ones who've influenced you most?" It was such an important question, and the fact that you asked it told me important things about you.

I love the way you describe your relationship with your aunt. I'm flattered—no, honored—that I remind you of her in any way. And not a little humbled. To have that kind of faith and courage!

Mary has told me you and your aunt always had a special connection and kept it going through the years. I'm sure your correspondence meant as much to her as it did to you. Did you keep the letters you wrote back and forth? There must be a wealth of wisdom in your interchanges. I can see your next book already. How about Letters for a Lifetime *as a title?*

Hmm... She could be right. He'd kept Aunt Liddy's letters over the years precisely because they did contain such insight and wisdom. George was perfect for him, Bronson mused—so in tune with him. So responsive. He continued to read:

I can identify with your feelings of "estrangement" from God. I've certainly been there. It's an encouraging word you've used, though—estranged. If you're estranged, you have felt close at some point in the past. And you can again.

Do you know John Donne's poetry? The sonnet that compares God's love to a compass? Not the kind that tells directions, but the kind a draftsman uses to draw circles. The point remains constant while the pencil moves closer or farther away—but always circling around the point. I like that picture, God holding on to us the way a compass holds a pencil, letting us wander, but never so far that we can't get back if we really want to.

My goal is to circle the point as closely as possible. To give myself in love and service to the God who created me and breathed his life into me, who is my teacher and my friend. What that means to me, in a practical sense, is using the gifts he's given me to make the world a better place.

A sharp mind, a tender heart—and a spirit as sensitive to God as his aunt's had been. George understood her life in the same way Aunt Liddy had, he thought. As a call to love and a call to serve.

I believe change happens in the world one person at a time, the letter went on. *God working through individuals to affect the lives of other individuals. You have a gift for language. And a love for language, I suspect. You have an opportunity to affect others profoundly with your words, and so to change the world.*

He stopped reading for a moment, stared unseeing out his apartment window. Change the world? He used to think his words had the power to change the world....

Stan had been as enthusiastic as he ever got over the articles he'd written about his experience with the group from Far East Adoptions—which was to say he complained about how long they were but didn't edit a single word.

He'd enjoyed writing the articles almost as much as he'd

enjoyed the trip. What a different experience than his last extended journey into China, when he'd done his research for the "Gone Missing" series.

For one thing, the orphanage in Fuzhou with which Far East Adoptions worked was a clean, bright facility in which the children were given not only excellent physical care but time, attention, and affection. The nursing supervisor, Li Jing Mei, was an exceptional young woman who had educated herself about early childhood development in a country where the entire concept of a pediatric specialty was foreign. The *amahs* she trained to look after the children knew what they were doing.

For another thing, Bronson couldn't remember the last time he'd been with a group of such upbeat, uncynical, genuinely caring people as the adopting parents he'd accompanied on their journey. His own cynicism softened in the face of their commitment to the babies they loved before they even held them in their arms. The evil in the world was great, but here and there a candle flickered in the darkness....

Was there still an idealist trapped inside his pessimism? Was it that hidden part of him that so resonated with Georgine?

His eyes returned to the page: *As for me,* she wrote, *I've always had a special love for children, and it's with children that my special gifts come out.*

For a while after my miscarriages and then the end of my marriage, I avoided children. They reminded me too much of my pain. But my life felt empty. Eventually, as God drew me closer to himself in my healing process, I started letting them back into my life. Now I have a marvelous time as a photographer of children for Child's Play.

Bronson frowned, feeling suddenly unsettled. Where was

she going with this train of thought? He read on:

It's time for the next step in my journey—and you've played a big part in my decision. Your gift for language has opened up a new way for me to use my gift for loving children. I've applied to adopt a child from China.

Thunderstruck wasn't nearly a strong enough term for his reaction to Georgine's words. *Hit by a bomb,* cliché that it was, described the effect more accurately.

It was as if he'd been strolling along a garden path, oblivious to everything but the light and warmth of a fine spring day, the color and fragrance of roses, the gentle touch of his lovely companion…then a flash, a scream, a boom, and a smoking hole where his dreams had been.

He read on, the pit opening wider inside him.

If I'd been aware of the option sooner, I'd probably have been a mother years ago. I'm thankful for the "coincidences" God has been arranging in my life in recent weeks to lead me to this decision, including meeting you and reading your article about abandoned baby girls in China.

And he'd doubted the power of his words!

I am as certain about taking this step as if God had spoken the words aloud, he read.

He closed his eyes, his heart in his stomach. How could she have made such a life-changing decision without consulting him?

"Consulting you!" His fist slammed down on the desk in frustration. "You've known her for a month, Bailey! You've never even kissed her! Why in the name of heaven and earth would she consult you?"

He got up, restless, and poured himself a glass of juice over ice, prowling the apartment while he drank it. But the letter drew him back. He focused his eyes again on her neat script:

My feelings are mixed as I write to you. I'm very excited about having a child in my life at last. But it's clear from your letter that choosing a child means not *choosing you.*

There it was in black and white. And she was right, of course. He'd made it clear he wasn't interested in children. Even thought it was a selling point, fool that he was. How could he not have taken into account Georgine's obvious affinity for children?

To be honest, he read on, *I'd been having some pretty wonderful fantasies about you and me and a little Chinese baby. I'm disappointed more than I would have thought possible after knowing you for such a short time.*

So he wasn't the only one...

We have completely different visions of our futures, Bronson. That's the bottom line. I wish things were different, but wishing can't make it so.

Bronson slumped down in his chair, staring once again out the window, unseeing.

It wasn't so much that their visions were different, he thought. It was that Georgine even had a vision. Did he?

Once upon a time he had. As a child, he'd had a vision of the life he was living now. Working as a journalist. Living in Asia.

Only now it wasn't enough.

Dreams needed to change as people changed. Grow as people outgrew them.

"Where there is no vision, the people perish," he murmured, the proverb surfacing from some long-ago sermon.

That was it.

He sat up straighter in his chair.

That was why he'd been so restless, felt so lost and alone these last few months. That was why his trip to Portland had acted like a shot in the arm: Aunt Liddy had given him a vision again. Reading the journals. Promising he would "do something" with them. A short-term vision, but a vision nevertheless.

He understood, suddenly, why he was so intensely disappointed with Georgine's decision to adopt a child. It was more than losing her.

She, too, had given him a vision. He'd imagined, for the first time in years, a life different than the one he lived now. Different in quality and substance. Different and better.

But his vision had not included a child.

He was almost fifty years old. He had written the truth in his letter to Georgine. He had no interest in children.

He'd also written the truth about feeling alive, connected, and full of hope since he'd met her.

He buried his face in his hands and bowed his head. "Dear God," he prayed, his voice sad, "I've moved so far away from you these last few years. Out at the farthest orbit, feeling as if you'd moved away from me instead of the other way around. Now I feel you pulling me in, through George, and Aunt Liddy, and those caring, committed people I traveled with in China. I feel the circles getting smaller. Closer in.

"I thought it was George I wanted—I suppose I still do. Or would, if things were different...

"But what I want even more than George is the kind of vision George has. The kind of vision Aunt Liddy had. A vision to love and to serve. Draw me closer to you. Open up new ways for me to use my gifts. Ways that please you. Ways that make the world a better place."

How difficult he'd made his life by losing himself in contemplation of man's cruelties instead of God's love—a love he could see when he looked for it. A love expressed through the care and commitment of people willing to get involved.

He wanted to be one of them.

"Teach me, Lord," he prayed. "Teach me, take me, open me, use me. Wherever you want.

"As for George—" He stopped, feeling helpless. "I don't know what to pray. She would be so easy for me to love...."

Once again he stopped, unsure. "Give her what her heart desires," he finally prayed. "Give her a child. Amen."

He lifted his head, taking a deep breath and letting it out slowly, more at peace than he could remember being in years.

I'm glad you got your leave of absence, Georgine's letter ended. *I know the book means a great deal to you. I do hope to hear about it as it progresses, but I'll understand if you'd prefer not to see me.*

In any case, I'll be praying for you. God is closer than you think. Warmest wishes, Georgine.

Prefer not to see her again? Bronson shook his head in wonder. If anything, he wanted to see her more. He didn't need a romance as much as he needed a friend, he told himself. And George was the kind of friend he needed.

She'd known how close God was. But she couldn't have known her letter would be the instrument of his own knowing.

Pulling out the stationery he'd bought exclusively for correspondence with Georgine, he once again set pen to paper and opened his heart.

On a steamy day in the last week of April, Bronson turned his office key over to his temporary replacement, an eager young man half his age who would cover the Asian beat for the *Los Angeles Examiner* for the next thirteen months. Or longer, if Bronson wasn't careful. He recognized ambition when he saw it.

His sabbatical would begin June 1, after a month's paid

vacation. He wasn't planning a vacation—being back in Oregon and starting on Aunt Liddy's book would be change enough to refresh him.

Double Happiness, Double Sorrow, his agent had suggested as a working title. He thought it a bit obscure, but he wasn't the marketing expert she obviously was; the advance she'd negotiated with a major publisher was astronomical. "That last award you won was like a red flag in front of a herd of bulls," she'd told him gleefully. "Everybody charged. You're a wanted man, Bronson Bailey."

"Yeah. Now let's hope I can deliver."

His agent wasn't worried, but Bronson had an anxious week when all he could think about was himself hunched over Aunt Liddy's journals and a keyboard, glassy-eyed, his behind glued to a chair for twelve months straight. He might be feeling burnt out with his current work, but it did combine physical and intellectual activities—travel, interviews, research, writing—in a balance that worked well for him. Sifting through the journals and deciding how to edit them would be intellectually stimulating, but he wondered if that would be enough.

By the end of the week he'd arranged two projects he was sure would break the monotony of working on the book day in and day out. One was with the director of Far East Adoptions and the other with his boss at the *Examiner.*

At least three or four times over the next year, he'd be escorting groups of adoptive parents as they met their children in China. The exact number and dates of the trips would depend on the number of clients the agency was serving and the ability of their Beijing connection to cut through the bureaucratic maze at the China Center of Adoption Affairs—the CCAA—at any given time.

Secondly—and he'd done some creative thinking and fast

talking to work this one out—he'd contracted with Stan to write a series of articles that would keep him in touch with Georgine on a regular basis.

He hadn't been sure what kind of reaction he'd get when he asked George to let him follow her through her adoption process for a series on international adoptions, but her return letter had been enthusiastic.

You're just the one to inspire people to think about adopting from overseas, she'd written. *I'd love to be part of your project.* She'd already started on the mountain of paperwork required by both the INS—the U.S. Immigration and Naturalization Service—and the Chinese government, but she promised to have copies of everything for him to look through.

Romance aside, Bronson thought as he boarded the plane for San Francisco later that evening, George would be good company for this crusty old bachelor. A most pleasant diversion...

He made his way down the aisle of the jumbo jet in an exceptional good humor, carrying a special gift for Georgine in his overnight bag and ignoring the nagging voice in his brain: *Careful, Bailey. Just watch that you don't fall in love.*

Eighteen

pril was a busy month for George. After sending her initial application to Far East Adoptions, she did the paperwork to take out a loan against her house for the adoption costs, got fingerprinted, and completed and mailed Form I-600A, "Application for Advance Processing of Orphan Petition," to the U.S. Immigration and Naturalization Service.

And she labored over what she believed might be the most important letter of her life—the letter that would eventually accompany her completed dossier to Beijing, addressed to the Officials of the People's Republic of China, explaining why she wished to adopt a child from their country. She worked on it for weeks, outlining, writing, revising, wanting it to be perfect, wanting the Chinese officials to know how loved her child would be.

Other prospective parents in George's preadoption classes were already ahead of her in the process, but when she considered she was only one person and still working more than full time at Child's Play, she decided she was doing as much as she could if she was to stay sane. And, as she quipped to Kim, since she wouldn't do a kid much good insane, she might as well accept her limitations.

At some point she was going to have to figure out what to do about reducing her workload, but for now she wanted to keep drawing her full salary and squirreling away as much as she could for the day she'd need the extra cash.

She and Kim had finished sorting through the fashion shots for the fall catalog and moved on to the next two steps in the process: scanning the selected photos into the Macintosh as low resolution black-and-white images and setting up the catalog pages on the computer, which included laying out the graphic elements and formatting the headlines and ad copy.

During the last week of the month she prepared several covers for the management team to choose from, one of them featuring her favorite shot of Maya Murphy. It was a shoe in at the team meeting at the end of the week.

At the same meeting, George lobbied for a Santa's workshop theme for the winter catalog over an outdoor sports theme, which would have required going out of town on location. She loved shooting on location, but her priorities had changed.

Since location shoots were expensive, Marty and Marilu had agreed without objections, and the rest of the team had fallen genially in line.

She felt good. She was doing fine. But there was still a mountain of paperwork to assemble for the adoption, and she was a little nervous about the home study she'd scheduled for the end of May—at the same time she'd be starting her shooting schedule for the winter catalog. Nervous because the home study, conducted by a state-licensed social worker, would determine her suitability as an adoptive parent.

Eileen Weintraub, the agency director, had assured her charges that this phase of the process was instructional, not punitive, and the homework she'd been giving them was designed to help them through it. George had read through the questions, but had not yet taken the time to sit down and think them through on paper: questions about her philosophy of child-rearing, her approach to discipline, the kind of relationship she'd had with her own parents—or, in her case, her aunt and uncle—growing up. Other questions about her financial stability, her plans for child care, her support system...

Bronson's call at the end of the month that he was back in town and would love to see her came at just the moment she'd decided she needed to schedule some fun before she turned into a pumpkin. Or worse, a drone. Dinner and a movie would be lovely...Chinese? Better yet.

A good thing he hadn't been as clear about his feelings in person before he left as he'd been in that letter, Georgine thought as she watched him bound up the sidewalk to her front door on Saturday night. And a good thing he'd been gone for seven weeks. Just looking at him did things to her insides. She wasn't sure her decision would have been as easy.

Why did it have to be that saying yes to one thing meant saying no to another? Especially when both choices had appeal? The worst of it was that until three months ago, she hadn't considered either a man or a child a likely addition to her life. So why had the perfect man—well, *almost* the perfect man—appeared in her life just at the time she realized a child was truly an option? Without a doubt, saying yes to Bronson would have meant saying no to a child.

Seeing him standing on her porch when she opened the front door sent her thoughts scrambling, and apparently, seeing her had the same effect on Bronson.

Neither of them said a word. Neither of them moved. She stood with her hand on the doorknob, with what she was sure must be a silly grin lighting her face. He stood in front of her with a brown paper package in his hands and a grin on his face as goofy as hers felt.

When they finally did speak, of course, they started at the same time, stopped, urged the other to go ahead, and then both burst into laughter.

"You look great, Georgine," Bronson finally got out as she let him into the house. She felt the appreciation in his glance and knew in that moment that she'd dressed tonight for him. The silk jacquard pantsuit, with its loose mandarin-collared top and flowing slacks, had elegant lines, and the deep turquoise did nice things for her skin.

So why was she dressing for Bronson Bailey?

"Looking pretty good yourself," she said, ignoring the nagging question. He was wearing dark gray slacks and a black sports jacket over a shirt the exact silver-gray of his eyes. And knotted firmly around his neck was the Curious George tie he'd worn to her office the day he'd come to visit.

"When did you buy that tie?" she asked. "I'm *curious*," she added, her smile mischievous.

"After I met you, but before I knew you were going to break my heart," he said.

"Right. You look pretty brokenhearted to me," she returned, her tone light. Then, more serious, "I'm glad we got all that— business—straightened out before you came back, Bronson. We might either one of us have been badly hurt."

"Rather than merely bitterly disappointed."

She laughed. "I must say I was a *little* hurt how easily you took my 'Dear John' letter."

"The sweetest, most sincere 'Dear John' letter it's ever been my privilege to receive," he said, a glint in his eyes. He sat down on the sofa at her silent invitation. "But seriously, George—as I wrote to you, that letter opened my eyes to the issues I'd been grappling with internally. Things have felt different since then."

"I'm glad, Bronson."

"It's incredible how God has used us in each other's lives in such important ways. And how we find ourselves at such different places, and yet such similar ones."

George sat down across the coffee table from him. "How do you mean?"

"Your last letter—how you've drawn so much of your sense of security from your work, from giving yourself so wholly to it, and how you're contemplating having to give that up in order to make room in your life for a child. Which reminds me—"

He handed her the package. "Something I found in Hong Kong before I left. I thought you might need it over the next few months, while you're waiting."

"I wondered if that package was for me," George said. "But you had such a death grip on it, I didn't want to chance taking it away."

"Yeah, yeah. Anyway—about security and work. I've been pretty attached to my career, and it feels a bit precarious to be leaving the *Examiner* behind even for a year. Maybe because I have this feeling I could be leaving it behind forever, and unlike you, I don't know why. What am I making room for in my life? Aunt Liddy's book for now, but what then? Because I know I don't want to go back to life the way it was a few short months ago, security or not."

"Exactly," George agreed. How was it that he understood so well?

The brown paper fell away from Bronson's gift to reveal a layer of bubble wrap, but she could see through the translucent layers what looked like a doll. *A doll?* she thought, puzzled. What an odd gift for a forty-nine-year-old man to bring a woman of thirty-nine...

She unwound the bubble wrap and let it drop to the floor. Her breath caught in her throat. She'd been right; it was a doll. A baby doll with almond eyes, rosebud lips, straight black hair, and golden skin. The bisque porcelain features were exquisitely painted, the cloth body dressed in beautifully detailed red silk pajamas.

"Oh, Bronson!" She cradled the baby in her arms.

"The adopting parents I escorted in March said the hardest part of the process was the waiting," he explained. "Most of them were married, so at least they had each other to turn to when the waiting got unbearable. I thought if you had something to hold on to during those times, something to remind you it was really going to happen…"

Tears sprang to her eyes.

Bronson nervously ran his fingers through his short, cropped hair. "I guess it was a stupid idea," he said.

"Oh, no! It's perfect. I'm just—overwhelmed." George hugged the doll close. "That you would know how special this would be."

"I didn't know. I—" He shrugged awkwardly. "I thought a china doll to hold on to would make it easier. Until you get the real thing," he finished, looking embarrassed.

"Thank you," she said, simply. It wasn't the doll itself that moved her, she realized. It was what the doll meant. It was Bronson saying he stood behind her, he believed in her vision, he would be there when the days grew long.

"So…" Bronson got up from the edge of the sofa. "Ready to go?"

"I'm ready to go," she said, smiling as she settled the doll on the chair and rose. "What more could you want your first night back from Hong Kong than Chinese dinner and a Chinese movie?"

"*American* Chinese dinner and a movie subtitled in English," he corrected her cheerfully. "And with a beautiful woman instead of alone." He waggled his eyebrows. "A different experience, believe me."

"Oh, Bronson—" She stopped, not sure how to respond to his flirtatious teasing when there was no place for it to go.

Just enjoy it, came the thought. *He obviously is.*

"I believe you," she said, throwing him an impish grin. "You have one of those faces even a mother could trust."

She grabbed her coat from the tree in the hallway and opened the front door. "Ready to paint the town red?"

Nineteen

Bronson realized after his first week back from Hong Kong he was spending far too much time with Georgine. Research, he'd excused himself at first as he delved into her thoughts about her decision to adopt from China.

But the fact was, the more he knew about her, the more he wanted to know, and his interviews always seemed to develop into events that felt amazingly like dates. Not that any of their times together ended in anything more than a kiss on the cheek.

As if he'd ever ended any other interview with a kiss on the cheek, he thought. The image of himself pecking at some dour Chinese bureaucrat's jowl lifted his mouth in a crooked smile.

He cut his calls back to once a week, sticking to the topic of the adoption over the phone, and saw George only on "official adoption" occasions: a couple of preadoption classes at Far East, which he audited for background information for his series, and her home study, conducted by a pleasant, pretty woman with a sharp mind and a soft voice.

Georgine had told him how intimidated she was about the social worker's visit, but she'd visibly relaxed as the home study progressed. "More like a friendly conversation than the inquisition I expected," she told him after the woman had gone. Still, he'd fixed her a soothing cup of tea before he left. Something any friend would do, he told himself.

After a month of living and working in the guest room at his sister's house, Bronson decided summer in the active household was not going to be conducive to getting any work done.

Editing Aunt Liddy's book was a very different project from anything he'd done before, and he was finding he needed more quiet than he was used to in order to give it his full attention. With Izzy and the twins still in school, he had a few good hours a day, but the afternoons and evenings when they were home gave him a vivid preview of how noisy summer was going to be.

He considered finding a furnished apartment in town, actually scanned the classifieds for a couple of weeks and checked out several possibilities, but in the end, no other place seemed as well suited to his purposes as his aunt's house on the Oregon coast. His and Mary's house now; Aunt Liddy had left the property jointly to Bronson and his sister. After a second trip to China in early June with another parent group from Far East Adoptions, he settled into Xi Jia Lou to get serious about his manuscript.

Not that he buried himself. He had coffee in a little cafe near the edge of town twice a week, where he flirted with the waitress and caught up on the local news; combined his weekly trip for groceries with a stop at the local library, where he caught up on the world and flirted with the librarian; and attended services at the Depoe Bay Bible Church, where he caught up on his faith and flirted equally with everyone, from babies to Aunt Liddy's contemporaries.

Aunt Liddy seemed as present in the town's memory and the house she'd loved as she was in her journals, a guiding spirit for his work. He was excited about the project, and it was going well.

With telephone service reconnected in the house, he could stay in touch with Georgine's adoption process for his *Examiner* series without having to be there, breathing down her neck.

Trouble was, he *wanted* to be there, breathing down her neck.

If they'd only had more time together up front, he thought. Why hadn't he kissed her when he'd had the opportunity, that night after dinner at the Tidal Rave? The way she'd looked at him, he'd known she wouldn't have said no.

It only would have made things harder, he argued with himself. Especially if the kiss had kindled anything close to the energy that arced between them when they talked. When they looked into each other's eyes...

Your imagination's gone into overdrive, Bailey, he scoffed at his fantasies. A kiss was just a kiss. He was obsessed with her because he couldn't have her—the old apple-in-the-center-of-the-garden syndrome.

Still...

All he needed was one kiss, he told himself. Proof there wasn't anything between them any more special than there'd ever been with anyone. Then he'd be able to get her out of his system.

At least he told himself that's why he wanted to kiss her.

Because he needed to get her out of his system. He had no future with Georgine and the child she was well on her way to making a permanent part of her life.

But she had him thinking things that weren't like him at all. After reading her stirring letter to the officials of the CCAA, he'd even tried to manufacture some interest in being a father. Or at least convince himself Georgine's desire for a child was strong enough for both of them. It didn't work. He couldn't put himself in the picture.

It would take a miracle.

One day when he'd wakened with Georgine on his mind and found her image still haunting him as he wrapped up a chapter of the book in early afternoon, he wandered restlessly onto the deck overlooking the sea, trying to shake her. He stared at the horizon for a moment, then wandered back through the house and stood on the front stoop, hands buried in his pockets, gazing around the overgrown garden.

A stucco wall in need of a fresh coat of paint, but otherwise in fair condition, surrounded the yard. A white lattice gate to one side led to the driveway. A "moon-gate," so called for its graceful, full-circle design, opened to the street in front of the house. Within the walls, Aunt Liddy had created a miniature garden in the classical Chinese style. Bronson remembered the contented hours she'd spent perfecting and maintaining it over the years, until, apparently, the effort had become too much for her.

The garden tools hung neatly on hooks at the side of the house, and on an impulse he grabbed a rake and set to work on the tangle of weeds. The physical labor was satisfying; for a few hours he lost himself in its rhythm, and the voices of Georgine Nichols and Aunt Liddy and Weldon Knight and, most of all, Bronson Bailey, fell silent in his head.

From then on he tried to spend at least an hour a day in the yard, cleaning up more than gardening, uncovering and discovering a design too well executed for simple neglect to have destroyed. Meanwhile he hired someone to put a fresh coat of white paint on the house and the garden wall, and one Saturday in early August he took a paintbrush to the moongate himself—red, for good luck and happiness, as Aunt Liddy herself had painted it.

He continued to call George weekly, monitoring her progress on the adoption and offering gentle reassurance when she sounded especially tired or discouraged. From the beginning of May through the end of July, while she and Kim put together the Christmas catalog for Child's Play, she ran herself ragged gathering the documents required by the INS and the

Chinese government for the adoption to proceed.

A month after her interview with the social worker, she received the completed home study and mailed it off to the Immigration and Naturalization Service. Another month and she'd received the coveted INS Form I-171H with its tongue-twisting title: Notice of Favorable Determination Concerning Application for Advanced Processing of Orphan Petition. Her application had been approved, at least on this side of the Pacific.

During those months she'd also been writing, making phone calls, and standing in line after line after line to get notarized copies of her birth certificate and her divorce decree and letters from her doctor, her bank, her employer, and the local police department, guaranteeing her physical and fiscal health and her lack of a criminal record. She'd taken photos of her house, inside and out, and had a friend take pictures of her. She'd asked Mary, Kim, and Toni to write personal letters of reference.

Gathering the documents together wasn't the end of it. Most of the paperwork had to be notarized. And certified. And authenticated. By early October, when the adoption agency finally forwarded her completed dossier to the China Center of Adoption Affairs in Beijing—in the company of a large stack of similar dossiers compiled with the same painstaking attention to detail as Georgine's—many of the items in her file had been through the hands of three separate secretaries of state and two Chinese consulate-generals.

And by that time, the Child's Play Christmas catalog was stacked in the warehouse ready for shipping, and George had only a few stills left to photograph for the spring catalog before the layout process began.

"I can't believe your energy," Bronson told her over the

phone, as if discounting his own: he'd written two articles in his series on international adoption, escorted yet another group of adopting parents to China in September, and was almost halfway through Aunt Liddy's journals. "I don't think you'll have any trouble at all keeping up with a kid," he teased.

"I'm not so sure you'd be using the word *energy* if you could see me right now," George replied. "And unless I make some drastic changes in my lifestyle, there's no *way* I'm going to keep up with a kid."

"Not getting cold feet, are you?" he asked, half hoping for selfish reasons her answer would be yes. But only half hoping; he knew how much George wanted this. Why wouldn't he want her to realize her dream?

Maybe because it gets in the way of yours…

"No cold feet," she said. "But I'm really tired. It worries me a little."

"You need a break," he said. "Why don't you come out for a couple of days?"

He held his breath. Where had that come from? He'd spent months purposely keeping his distance, and now he was inviting her to—to what? What would she infer from his invitation? She was taking her time to answer…

"Not here," he added hastily. "I mean, not with me. Didn't you say you have friends who own a unit at the Inn at Otter Crest?"

"Maybe it's open sometime in the next couple of weeks," she said, but her tone was doubtful. "I don't know, Bronson. I've really got to come up with some kind of workable plan for my job. Marty and Marilu need to make some decisions."

"So do you," he said. "You need a change of pace, Georgine. A fresh look at things. Besides," he coaxed, committed now to the idea his subconscious had produced, "I promised you a long time ago I'd show you Xi Jia Lou."

"I would like to see that garden you've been raving about," she mused.

He pulled out his final gun. "It's my fiftieth birthday next week," he admitted. "I'd rather not spend it alone."

"Really? My fortieth's the week after next!"

"That settles it, then. We'll make it a double birthday bash—we can take each other out to dinner."

What was it that made her hesitate? And more important, perhaps—what was it that made her give in a moment later?

"All right," she said. "I'll check with Clark and Toni. If their condo isn't available, I can stay in one of the rental units. You're right—it would do me a world of good to have a change of scenery about now. I'll give you a call next week, okay?"

Before he had a chance to grab it and hold it down, his heart had soared away. "Great!"

"Great," he repeated to himself when he'd hung up the phone, but this time his tone was less enthusiastic.

What was he getting himself into?

A perfectly lovely weekend, as it turned out.

"I don't want to talk about work, and I don't want to talk about the adoption," Georgine had told him firmly when she'd called back to confirm her plans. "If I start to say anything about either, stop me."

"You're sure?"

"I'm sure. Promise?"

"Promise. We don't have to talk about anything. We'll eat, and walk on the beach, and eat, and maybe go to the Oregon Coast Aquarium, and eat—"

"The aquarium!" she interrupted. "I've been wanting to see Keiko, after all the fuss."

"I'll show you Keiko, and a stunning colony of jellyfish, and otters and puffins and a little fish whose species I can't remember but I call Admiral Buttons—"

"I know the one! He looks as if he's wearing a brass-buttoned jacket, and he stares with such condescension and authority."

He grinned. This was going to be fun. "We may even have to make the rounds of the factory outlet stores in Lincoln City," he added. "I've heard there's nothing like a good shopping spree to get a woman's mind off just about anything."

"You have, have you? And where would an old bachelor have learned a thing like that?"

"You calling me old?" he teased instead of answering the question.

Their cheerful bantering over the phone set the stage for the weekend. She didn't get out to the coast till late Friday night, but bright and early Saturday morning he picked her up in the lobby at the Inn at Otter Crest and drove to Newport, where they found a breakfast café, ate blueberry pancakes, and read the Portland morning edition, sharing interesting tidbits back and forth.

Then they spent hours at the aquarium, delighting in the diversity and whimsy of the beasts in God's creation. They came face to face through thick plate glass with Keiko, the killer whale who was a movie star; stood hypnotized in front of the jellyfish display, where the graceful creatures were illumined with soft colored lights; laughed at a pair of sea otters lying on their backs in their water tank, holding flippers.

And they ended their day back in Depoe Bay, at the Tidal Rave, where Bronson kept her to her word, and they discussed books, music, movies, and childhood memories with nary a word about her work or her adoption.

He'd told her not to get him a birthday gift, but he had one for her, picked up on his last trip to China to give her at Christmas: a strand of freshwater pearls in a tiny, silk brocade purse. He'd have to come up with something else for Christmas.

"Bronson, it's too much!" she protested, fingering the strand. "But they're beautiful." She closed her fingers around them, smiling at him.

Not as beautiful as you are, he thought. "Let me put them on for you," he said, getting out of his chair at the restaurant to move behind her, fumbling with the clasp as she held her hair up off her slender neck.

"There." He settled the pearls around her neck, then lightly smoothed his hands along her shoulders as she let her hair fall back into place. He felt her go still.

And in her stillness, he understood the power his touch held over her, and the power her response held over him.

God, help me, he prayed. *I cannot seem to help myself.*

Twenty

Georgine couldn't remember another time in the last six months she'd felt so completely relaxed. Not wanting to lose momentum in an adoption process that took a year even when everything ran smoothly, she'd pushed herself hard. Leisure had been measured in moments rather than hours or days while she worked on compiling her dossier and tried to maintain her standards of excellence for the Child's Play publications.

She'd forgotten how important leisure was in the creative process. All day Saturday and all through the night, while she'd consciously turned off her thoughts about her priority concern—how she was going to balance her job and her family life—her subconscious had been hard at work untying the knotty problem.

The solution she'd come up with was risky, but no more a risk than those she'd taken in the past with her career. Leaving her first job as a house-paid wedding photographer to strike out on her own in the fashion industry had been a risk. Leaving a very successful freelance career in fashion photography to take the job as creative director at Child's Play had been a risk. Now, leaving the security of a monthly paycheck to go freelance again would be a risk.

But she would be focusing on the part of her work she liked best—standing behind the camera. And she was pretty sure, considering the awards her catalogs had won, she could negotiate a contract with Marilu and Marty to continue providing the bulk of their photography needs, and maybe some ongoing consulting services.

She'd recommend the hiring of a graphic artist to design the catalogs, and the creation of a new position for Kim as manager of catalog production. That would technically make Kim her boss, but since the two worked more as partners than as boss and employee now, she didn't think their relationship would change much. It was bringing a third person into the mix she worried about more. Finding the right person for the design work could be a challenge.

But that had nothing to do with today, she told herself as she checked her reflection in the mirror before walking down to wait for Bronson. He'd promised to collect her in time for the worship service at Depoe Bay Bible Church, and then take her to Xi Jia Lou for Chinese stir fry and a tour of his Aunt Liddy's house and garden. It felt appropriate to wear the slim coral silk dress she'd brought with her, with its mandarin collar and braided frog fasteners.

She didn't look the slightest bit Chinese in any other way, with her height, and her pale hair pulled back in a sleek chignon, and her Indo-European facial features. Features which to an Asian must seem sharp and pointed and not particularly attractive, she thought. She wondered if she looked that way to Bronson—sharp and pointed. He'd lived in an Asian culture for so many years.

She scrutinized her reflection in the mirror. Maybe she looked different to him, she mused, but definitely not unattractive. The way he looked at her made that very clear.

The thought changed her image in the mirror almost imperceptibly: a little added color to her cheeks, an extra glimmer to her dark brown eyes, an air of buoyancy. Expectancy. She and Bronson...

Could he be coming around to the idea of having a child? He'd be a wonderful father, she told herself as she walked down the winding drive to the lobby to wait for him. Just the right balance of work and play, authority and tenderness, responsibility and delight. The best of fathers—if he wanted to be.

She put the thought out of her mind. Whatever else Bronson Bailey did or didn't want, he wanted to be with her today. And she wanted another day like yesterday: relaxed, carefree, leisurely, in the company of a good friend. For whatever else Bronson Bailey was or wasn't, he was her friend.

She recognized several people who greeted them when they walked into the little church: the minister and some of the women she'd worked beside at the reception after Lydia Bronson's memorial service. But it was clear Bronson was the real reason for their friendliness and curiosity.

So he'd been setting hearts aflutter over the last few months, she thought with amusement. No surprise; he'd set her own aflutter, months ago, the first time she'd seen him. In this very place.

She liked sharing the hymnbook with him, enjoyed harmonizing as he carried the melody in a strong baritone. She liked being with him here, sitting close, as if they were a couple, as if they belonged on the pew next to each other....

Careful, she told herself. *Don't spoil what you have by wanting too much more.*

But the sermon, based on a familiar and well-loved passage from the Psalms, didn't help suppress her dreams at all.

Trust in the LORD and do good;
>   dwell in the land and enjoy safe pasture.
Delight yourself in the LORD
>   and he will give you the desires of your heart.

Commit your way to the LORD;
   trust in him and he will do this:
He will make your righteousness shine like the dawn,
   the justice of your cause like the noonday sun.

Was God telling her she could have Bronson as well as a baby?

She sneaked a look at him and found that he was frowning in concentration.

He didn't say much on the ride to the beach house after church, but then, neither did she. There was a difference in their silences, though. Hers was thoughtful, reflective; his made him seem utterly remote.

"What are you thinking?" she finally asked as they turned onto a gravel road off Otter Crest Loop.

She could see her question startled him. He glanced briefly at her, then back to the road. His frown relaxed, but not the tension in his arms and back. "I'm sorry—I was a million miles away, wasn't I?" But he didn't answer her question.

A moment later he stopped the truck.

From her first view of Xi Jia Lou, Georgine was entranced. Behind the high wall with its elegant red moon-gate, through the lacy lobes of a spindly red-leaf maple and the delicate leaves of a bamboo grove, a gray roof rose over a long, low-slung house painted the same fresh white as the wall which surrounded it. With its slender pillars, beams, and crosspieces painted jet black, it looked like a Chinese ink-and-wash painting against the blue sky and the trio of pines rising beyond the roofline.

"The painters did a good job," Bronson said as he opened the gate and ushered her into the yard.

She stopped abruptly. "So did the gardener," she said in awe as he closed the gate and latched it.

"Aunt Liddy, not me," he said, standing close behind her. "She was the artist. I just dug it out from under the weeds." He pointed beyond a mound where an apricot tree grew, ripe with fruit, to one side of the garden. "There's a straight path to the front door from a gate over there along the driveway, but walking this one makes you feel as if the house sits a quarter mile back from the road."

She understood what he meant as she followed the stone walkway winding from the moon-gate to the front door, stopping after every curve in the path to gaze around in wonder, surprised by every new vista revealed. Plants, rocks, water, grassy hillocks—everything was arranged to create an illusion of depth and spaciousness in the small garden.

Around one bend water trickled over and through a pile of artfully arranged rocks into a pool, like a river spilling down a mountainside to a lake. The banks of the pond twisted and turned to form spits, inlets, and bays.

"Like a landscape in miniature," George said, enthralled.

Bronson nodded. "Like a dozen landscapes in miniature. A new one with every turn. Aunt Liddy used to say that Chinese gardens are like three-dimensional pictures, and the path is like a tour guide that invites you in and shows you around."

"A perfect metaphor."

Across a wooden bridge around another bend, the path led down a short flight of steps, created from stone slabs set into the hillside, to a secluded nook where a stone bench overlooked the sea.

She sat down, leaving room for Bronson, but he remained standing, staring out to sea. He still seemed remote. She recalled Mary's initial description of her brother as aloof, and for the first time understood her friend's experience of Bronson.

Why had he responded so warmly to her, from the very beginning? And why was he not, now?

She closed her eyes and took a deep breath, refusing to let his moodiness affect her good spirits. The scent of pine mingled with the distinctive smell of the sea, salty and astringent. The sun warmed her face, and with the roar of the waves in the distance she could hear the trickling water of the stream behind her and the soughing of the wind through the pines. Aunt Liddy's garden was a treat for all the senses.

"It's lovely every season of the year," Bronson interrupted the silence. "She always told me what was happening in the garden when she wrote. Apricot blossoms in the spring, water lilies in summer, leaves turning color in the fall, the sound of rain on plantain leaves on a stormy winter day."

"Mmm. Good stuff for that book of correspondence between you and your aunt," George said with a smile, opening her eyes. He looked at her, really looked at her, and his remoteness fell away with his own smile, warm and genuine.

"I've been thinking about that one," he said. He reached out a hand to help her up and kept his fingers wrapped around hers as he pulled her up the sloping path to the house. "Hungry?"

"Getting there. Do you need help, or could I spend some time in the garden with my camera?"

"I prepped my vegetables this morning before church, so there isn't much left to do for dinner. Shoot away," he answered.

A series of photos of the house and garden for Bronson to take back to Hong Kong when he left would be a perfect birthday gift, she thought as she followed the winding path once again from the moon-gate to the house, clicking away. By the time he called her in for dinner, she'd shot two rolls of film.

She'd always liked Asian food, but usually ate it out, in one of Portland's many excellent Chinese or Thai restaurants. Bronson's Chinese was delicious: egg-flower soup, shrimp-fried rice, cashew chicken, steamed bok choy, rice noodles.

The afternoon flew by. Bronson took her back to the condo, where she changed into jeans and a sweater and windbreaker for a walk on the beach. Back at Xi Jia Lou, they sat on the deck, adding layers of clothing as the sun slipped westward, while Bronson read aloud from his manuscript, hanging on to the pages in the wind.

When it got too dark to read, they sat in companionable silence, sipping at mugs of hot chocolate while they watched the sun bury itself in the sea. "The House of Evening Splendor," George said softly as the light faded from the sky. "Thanks for sharing it with me, Bronson. And for sharing your work with me."

The conversation he was creating between his aunt and Weldon Knight from her journals and his letters was fascinating stuff. In the midst of cataclysmic social and political change in China, and with it a great deal of anti-Western sentiment, their very survival seemed a miracle. That they survived while loving and humbly serving a people through years of uncertainty and upheaval spoke profoundly of their faith.

"Except that Dr. Knight didn't survive," George reminded Bronson.

"No. I still wonder, if he had, if I might not have grown up with another entire set of cousins...."

"Mary told me once your aunt felt that every child she worked with as a nurse and educator was her child," George said. "That she didn't need to have a child of her own because every child was hers. Do you think that was really true?"

"I don't know. I know she loved children. She loved people. Why?"

"Because I've tried that, too. With my friends' kids, and the kids I photograph. Tried to feel as if they were mine, I mean." She shook her head. "Maybe my heart's not as big as your Aunt Liddy's was. Other people's children—it's just not the same."

He reached across the space between their deck chairs and took her hand. "Your heart is beautiful, Georgine," he said, his voice tender. "Don't abuse it."

A lump rose in her throat. She couldn't have answered if she'd known what to say.

He was quiet for a moment. "One of the last things Aunt Liddy said to me before she died was that she cried when she delivered me because I wasn't hers," he said, squeezing her hand. "I think she grieved her childlessness, and then I think she let it go."

"And do you think I'm weak because I haven't let it go? Because I'm not accepting childlessness?" Her throat felt suddenly tight with emotion. She didn't know why she'd asked him such a question, put him in such an awkward position.

But his answer came without hesitation. "No. I think you are as strong in your own way as Aunt Liddy was in hers."

She felt the tension in her throat release. "Thank you," she whispered, entwining her fingers with his.

She turned her head and met his eyes in the dusk, and she knew what he was going to do. And she knew she wasn't going to stop him.

It had been so long since she'd been kissed. So long since she'd wanted to be.

He was gentle with her. Sweet. She closed her eyes, savoring the feeling of his lips on hers, the warmth of his hands on her arms, and when he started to pull away, without conscious thought she lifted her hand to the back of his head and pulled him back.

For an instant fire leapt between them. Then Bronson jerked away.

"George." His voice was strangled. "We mustn't."

She recoiled as if he'd slapped her. "No. Of course not," she said after a moment, her voice dull. What had she been thinking? He'd only meant to comfort her with his kiss. She'd taken it all wrong, forced it into something it wasn't meant to be. "I'm sorry."

"No, it's my fault, I didn't mean—I'm sorry, George. I never want to do anything to jeopardize our friendship. It's too important to me." He sounded genuinely anguished.

"Is it?" she asked quietly.

"You understand me in ways no one else does, Georgine. Now that Aunt Liddy's gone—" He stopped, shaking his head. "You were right from the beginning, about our lives being on different tracks," he said. "But I treasure our friendship. Yes. It's very important to me."

She was a replacement for his ninety-year-old aunt. When she stopped feeling mortified, she was going to have a great laugh about this. Maybe someday she'd even tell Mary.

But not for a good long while yet.

"Am I forgiven?"

She reached across to take his hand again, squeezed it, let it drop. He hadn't misled her. She'd simply let the beauty and the romance of the place carry her away. "There's nothing to forgive. And Bronson—your friendship is important to me, too. This weekend has been wonderful. Thank you."

Maybe this needed to happen, she told herself as she drove back to Portland in the dark. Maybe now she could lay her fantasies about Bronson Bailey to rest.

Twenty-one

In truth, Bronson had been shattered by the kiss.

In that instant when Georgine had pulled him back and fireworks had exploded in his head, everything had changed. He would never again be able to fool himself that what existed between them wasn't special.

The kiss had told him what his heart already knew. His mind had worked hard trying to talk his heart out of it these last few months, but that was over now. His mind was convinced as well.

He loved her.

And because he loved her, he had to pretend he didn't.

He knew from her response to his kiss that his feelings were reciprocated. He guessed, from what Mary had told him and from Georgine's earliest responses to his touch, that she hadn't kissed a man the way she'd kissed him for a very long time. And she couldn't afford to get mixed up with him now, when the wheels were already in motion for Beijing to assign her a child. If she didn't know that—well, he did. He was the only one who could protect her from himself.

She'd already made her choice. And as much as it pained him to acknowledge it, he knew it was the right choice for her. If he hadn't known it before, he knew it after that last conversation. *"Other people's children have never felt like they were mine." "Do you think I'm weak because I'm not accepting childlessness?"* With longing in her voice—a yearning so deep he hadn't been able to resist the need to comfort her…

But he discovered in the next few weeks he couldn't bear to

be away from her, either. More than ever now he missed her company: her eagerness for adventure, her sharp mind, her sense of humor, her warm eyes and bright smile.

He drove to Portland for Thanksgiving at his sister's house knowing George would be there and proved to himself he was better off around her in the role of friend than not seeing her at all. After a third trip to China for Far East Adoptions in early December, he closed up the house in Depoe Bay and moved into the basement apartment of an elderly widow from Mark and Mary's church before Christmas.

"Too dreary for you at the coast once winter set in?" George asked him sympathetically when he called to say he was living in Portland.

"Too lonely."

"What?" she needled. "With all those ladies at the church so curious and interested?"

"But none as interesting as you, Curious George," he said, his tone deliberately teasing.

He was relieved when she laughed, taking his comment as lightly as he'd hoped she would. Even though the words were from his heart.

"How's the book coming?" she asked.

"Good. It's practically writing itself. I think I'll be done before my last trip to China for the agency. Sometime in March."

"Your last?"

"My sabbatical's over June first. I doubt there'll be another trip before then."

She was silent for a long moment. Would she miss him when he was gone?

When she spoke, her voice was wistful. "Maybe I'll be on that one with you."

His heart skipped a beat at the thought. Taking George to see the Great Wall, the Forbidden City, Drum Mountain...

"Maybe," was all he said.

"I know it's too soon, but I keep waiting for a call from the agency," she admitted. "You were right about the waiting being the hardest part."

"I'm praying for you."

"Thanks. That means a lot."

"How are things at work?" he asked. "The new graphics guy working out?" She'd told him at Thanksgiving that she'd hired a graphic artist to handle the catalog design and was taking him through the entire summer catalog cycle to train him. In the spring, she'd be looking over his shoulder while he did the work, and by the time May rolled around, the catalog design for the Christmas issue would be his baby. And, if dreams could be counted on, George would have a baby of her own.

"He's very talented," she said. "But I'm not too sure about the chemistry between him and Kim—he has that notorious artistic temperament, and Kim doesn't put up with much of that."

"So how'd you escape the curse of the artistic temperament? You seem so even-keeled."

"I didn't escape it. I'm not a prima donna, and you won't find me flying into rages, but I can sure cry up a storm," she said.

He winced to think about her crying. Especially alone...

He sat with her at the Christmas Eve service at Tomahawk Community Church, and spent Christmas Day in her company—along with Mary, Mark, all seven of their children, and the three granddaughters: Elizabeth, five; Annie, two; and Brittany, who was only six months old.

The jealousy that flashed through him just for an instant as he watched George play with the baby frankly astonished him. For all his awareness of his feelings about Georgine, he hadn't realized jealousy was part of the mix.

He wanted to be as important to her as children were. He wasn't. Nothing could change the fact of her choice.

Keep me from resentment, Lord.

She was delighted with the book and video he'd given her for Christmas, a copy of Pearl Buck's *The Good Earth* and the classic Ingrid Bergman movie, *Inn of the Sixth Happiness,* the true story of a missionary to China who'd been a contemporary of his aunt. Her gift for him was just as carefully selected: a leather-bound copy of the poetry of John Donne, the bookmark set at the sonnet she'd described to him in her first letter to Hong Kong.

His walk with God had changed since he'd received that letter, he reflected. He'd realized his feelings of estrangement were a result of his holding back from God, not the other way around. He still felt as if he were walking blind, but at least he knew someone was there in the dark with him—someone whose eyes could penetrate the darkest night. Someone who could lead him through it.

He and Georgine saw each other often after that: always at church on Sundays and once or twice during the week to share a meal, a movie, a winter walk at the Grotto or at Crystal Springs Garden, close to his apartment near Reed College. George had told the truth about enjoying walks in the rain, and in late January when cold weather finally hit, he discovered she liked walking in the snow even better.

He could be with her when he could let the moment be enough. His future was still dark, but she illuminated his present. There was something to be said for living fully in the present and leaving the future in the hands of a God who could see the broad picture, he told himself. A God who knew him better than he knew himself.

Or was he only in denial?

Beijing still hadn't assigned Georgine a child by the time Bronson made his fourth trip to China on behalf of Far East Adoptions in mid-March. She'd tried to be philosophical about it, but the disappointment in her eyes had given her away. Those eyes haunted him the entire two weeks he was gone.

The last night of the trip, as he left the restaurant at the Eaton Hotel in Hong Kong with several members of the Far East group, he caught a fleeting glimpse of a lovely blonde before her head dipped behind a menu at a table set for one.

He stopped short. Georgine? What in the world was she doing in Hong Kong? Alone?

She set the menu down and reached a graceful arm for her water glass, and suddenly Bronson realized his mistake—the same mistake he'd made the first time he'd seen George.

It was Pamela.

He pulled out the chair across from her and sat down, watching her expression change from surprise to pleasure. Certainly more pleasure than she'd expressed the last time he'd seen her, more than a year ago now. Last year's Chinese New Year. He remembered how cool and distant she'd seemed. No surprise after she'd broken her news.

"Bronson! Bronson Bailey, you are an absolute wretch!"

He laughed. "It's nice to see you, too, my dear. Looking as elegant as ever. So what have I done now?"

"Oh, nothing much. Left town without a word about it, didn't write, didn't leave an address. Where *have* you been?"

"Oregon. Writing a book. And how do you think I felt when you announced you were going to marry a man I hadn't even met?" He pretended to be aggrieved. "As if you didn't care a whit whether or not I approved?"

Pamela sighed. "Maybe I should have waited for your stamp of approval. Maybe I should have waited for *you.*"

He searched her face, frowning. "What do you mean? He hasn't been treating you well?"

"I mean he hasn't been treating me, period. I broke the engagement last summer." She tilted her head to one side and gave him a coquettish smile. "Why do you think I was so frantic to find you?" She sighed again, the smile dissolving into tired lines around her mouth. Unhappiness had made itself at home on her face since he'd seen her last, he thought.

"Did you check in at the office?"

She nodded. "The snotty-nosed kid who took your place said if I really wanted to reach you I could write to the *Examiner.*"

"I wish you had. I'm sorry, Pamela. It must have been hard."

Her expression was grateful. "Yes. Thank you. You wouldn't believe how many people have said, 'Why are *you* upset? *You're* the one who broke the engagement.'"

"Still, something important to you ended. Grief is the natural reaction," he said quietly.

She looked startled. "Yes. Thank you," she said again.

He hesitated, wondering if he should ask about the details. In all the years they'd known each other, he realized, they'd never talked about anything as personal as he and George had shared over the last few months.

But she looked so sad. "What happened?" he asked, his voice gentle.

He didn't know if she'd answer at first, but after a moment of staring off into the distance, she returned her eyes to his and said, "I just didn't see how I could make it work. He wanted a family, and he had me pretty well convinced that I did, too. But when it came down to giving up my job…I couldn't do it."

"But why would you have to give up your job?" he asked, thinking of the compromises George was making to accommodate both her work and a child. "Couldn't you have worked something out between the two of you?"

"It wasn't just that, Bronson." She hesitated, then quirked her lovely mouth in a self-deprecating grin. "You know me. I've never exactly been the nurturing type. Can you really see me making goo-goo eyes at a baby? Doing all that fussing mothers do?" She shook her head. "I'm almost forty. If the baby bug hasn't bit me yet, it ain't a-goin' to, honey."

She was trying to be lighthearted, but Bronson saw beneath it to her sadness. Thank God he hadn't let himself get as deeply involved with George as Pamela had been with her fiancé, he thought. It was hard enough as it was.

You think you're not deeply involved? He couldn't shut out the question.

"Shall I set another place, miss?"

He glanced up to see the majordomo with his head inclined to Pamela.

She looked at him. "Bronson?"

"I've eaten, but I'll have a drink while you have dinner. We have a lot of catching up to do."

It was easy being with her again, he thought. Comfortable. Just what he needed to take his mind off Georgine.…

"So you're not back in Hong Kong to stay," she said, her disappointment evident, after he told her why he was there.

"No. But I should be back by June."

She brightened. "That's not too far away. We've gone that long without seeing each other when we've both been living here."

"Why was that, anyway?" His voice was teasing.

"Bronson…"

He looked at her expectantly.

"Maybe you and I should try again."

He raised an eyebrow. "Did we ever really try?"

"I did. You…I can't say. But you seem different now."

"Different?" He drew his brows together in a frown. "How do you mean?"

"Softer. More compassionate." She grinned suddenly. "Not so bloody objective."

Answering her grin, he retorted, "Maybe you're the one who's changed. Maybe you're not so bloody critical." But he knew she was right. He was softer. Maybe it came from loving Georgine.…

"We understand each other, Bronson," Pamela said. "We want the same thing. I think we could be good."

Did she understand him? In the way Georgine did? Could she? "What is it we want?" he asked.

"Good companionship. Someone to unwind with. Maybe a little adventure. Simple enough."

Simple enough. He couldn't argue with her checklist. Certainly a year ago it would have felt complete.

Aunt Liddy suddenly came to mind. Before the trip, as projected, he'd finished his manuscript. In his spare minutes over the last two weeks he'd been working on the preface, reflecting on the legacy his aunt had left behind: the lives she'd touched through her gifts for love and service. Her unwavering faith in God.

And then Georgine came to mind, smiling at him with her warm brown eyes.

"Good companionship, someone to unwind with, a little adventure," he repeated slowly. "Simple enough." *But what about faith?* he thought. *What about love? What about contribution?*

"Think about it," she said. "Call me when you get back."

Later, back in his hotel room, Bronson lay awake until the early hours of the morning, his mind wrestling with the unanswered questions in his life, with the uncertainty of his future.

God, why did you bring Georgine into my life? his heart cried out. *Only to teach me? Did I need her to find my way back to you? And to prove to myself I'm capable of love?*

Maybe Pamela was the woman God had for him in the long term, he told himself. Maybe he was meant to love Pamela instead of Georgine.

Where do I go from here? he prayed, passionate in his desire to know. *Lord, what would you have me to do?*

Follow me, came the answer. *I will lead you.*

Twenty-two

A year after her initial decision to adopt, Georgine felt no closer to motherhood than ever. "No woman should have to be pregnant this long," she groused to Mary on a blustery day in early April. Rain spattered against the window at their favorite lunch spot. "And I still don't know how many months I have to go before I actually get to hold a baby in my arms and know she's mine."

"How long has Beijing had your dossier now?" Mary asked.

"Six months. Supposedly it takes about eight months from the time the CCAA gets the dossier till the baby is 'delivered.' It's been six, and I don't even have my child assignment yet." George sighed. "Last summer when I was trying to get all the paperwork together, I felt like I was racing inches ahead of an avalanche. Now I feel like I'm stranded on the side of the mountain like a lost soul."

"Not to worry. Here comes your Saint Bernard," Mary quipped, looking over George's shoulder. "For two people not dating, you and Bronson spend an awful lot of time together," she added.

George turned her head to follow Mary's gaze. Bronson was standing at the hostess desk scanning the room. His face lit up as their eyes met. He made a beeline for their table. "George! Kim told me she thought you'd be here."

"Hello, Bronson," Mary interjected.

"Hi, Mary," he said, but his eyes were only for Georgine. "I was at the Far East office this morning to debrief about my last trip. While I was there, twenty-three assignments came in.

George, you have a baby!"

She was out of her seat and in his arms almost before his words were out. She'd known the moment she saw his face something wonderful had happened. Bronson didn't get excited for nothing.

"Everyone's looking," he teased, his mouth against her ear as she hugged him, laughing and crying at the same time.

"Let them look." She pulled away, flinging one arm out as she held tightly to his hand with the other, and announced to the entire dining room, "I'm getting a baby!" There was a scattering of applause as she peppered Bronson with questions: "What's her name? What does she look like? When can I see her picture?"

He laughed and hugged her again. "My chariot awaits," he said. "Mary, want to come?"

"I wouldn't miss it!"

Ten minutes later they were in the agency's downtown office, Mary and Bronson sitting in the waiting area and Georgine pacing the carpet outside the director's door. "Eileen wants to talk over your assignment with you," the receptionist had told her.

She wouldn't have thought her statement odd except that when a couple she remembered from the preadoption classes rushed in a few minutes later, the girl brightly handed them a file folder and offered them congratulations. Why was George being made to wait? What was wrong? Her throat tightened with anxiety.

The office door opened and Eileen Weintraub stepped out. Her expression was serious. "Georgine, sorry to make you wait. Please, come in."

George glanced at Mary and Bronson. Eileen hesitated, then invited them in as well. She was aware of the series Bronson was writing, and knew Mary was a major player in George's circle of support.

"It looks as if the CCAA has made a mistake," she said without preamble after they all were seated. She fingered a file folder on her desk. "It happens sometimes."

George's heartbeat quickened. "My child assignment didn't come through."

"No, no, it did come through. But it's not what you requested."

She handed the folder to Georgine, who stared at it for a moment without lifting the cover.

"You don't have to accept the assignment," Eileen said. "You'd probably have another by tomorrow."

George felt a hand squeeze her shoulder. She darted Bronson a grateful look, then with a deep breath opened the folder.

Her eyes widened when she saw the picture inside. She glanced quickly at Eileen. "She's not a baby."

"No. I know you requested an infant, as young as possible. Yin Suyuan is almost fourteen months old."

"Suyuan?"

"Long-Cherished Wish," Bronson said softly beside her. "Her name means Long-Cherished Wish."

George's breath caught in her throat. *Long-Cherished Wish.* She studied the photo. A beautiful little girl stared back, her almond eyes mischievous under arched eyebrows, her sunny smile revealing four tiny teeth. Her black hair was cut stylishly short, with straight, thick bangs. Her Western-style dress was outlandishly frilly and frothy, parfait pink with roses appliquéd around the collar.

Mary, looking over her shoulder, read aloud the text that accompanied the picture. "Birthdate: February 11. Height: 33

inches; weight: 21 pounds; Hepatitis B: negative. Healthy girl. And listen to this: Suyuan likes to comb her hair, brush her teeth, eat meat, and drink milk. How funny. I wonder if they put the same thing on all the pictures." She studied the photo for a moment. "George, she's an absolute *doll.*"

George knew what she meant. But this was no doll, like the one Bronson had brought her from Hong Kong. This was a little person. Flesh and blood. A personality that almost jumped off the page.

She couldn't tear her eyes away from the photograph. *This is my little girl,* she thought with wonder. *My long-cherished wish...*

"She's perfect," she breathed. She looked at Eileen. "The CCAA might have made a mistake, but God didn't. I love her," she said, simply.

"You're sure?"

"I'm sure." She knew it was safer to adopt an infant than an older child, who might have suffered more from neglect or malnutrition. And it seemed ridiculous, loving someone on the basis of a picture. But there was no other way to describe her feelings. This was the child she'd been waiting for. Not just over the last six anxious months, but all her life.

Eileen smiled. "I hoped that would be the case, Georgine. I agree with you—sometimes it seems there's a higher power at work in the child assignments than the Chinese government. You don't know how often that word *perfect* comes up."

They stopped at a copy store on the way back, and George made a dozen color copies of Suyuan's profile, then another dozen copies "just in case." In case of what, she had no idea, but already she could think of a list of people she wanted to send the picture to. Her Aunt Ione—who had tried to talk her out of the adoption but came around when she realized how committed George was; several friends in San Diego she'd written to at Christmas about her plans; Kim and Felice at work; Toni, Katie, Emily....

"You both want one, right? 'Aunt' Mary and 'Uncle' Bron?" They grinned at her exuberance and told her of course they did, and she ought to send one to the neighborhood newspaper where she lived and post one on the "Family News" bulletin board at church and...

Eileen called a meeting the following week for the twenty-three families whose assignments had come through. The room was a nervous, noisy buzz, people sharing their children's pictures and profiles and conjecturing about their histories; repeating stories they'd heard about the finalization process for the adoptions, rumors about when they might be traveling to China, hints they'd picked up from the Internet about what to take and how to pack....

It was finally happening! They were going to be parents. The proof was in their hands.

As he had been for every step of George's adoption process, Bronson was there, making the rounds of the group, asking questions, gathering information. She watched him move easily around the room, interested, alert, curious, confident.

The series Bronson was writing was one of his own choosing, Georgine knew. She still didn't know if he'd chosen it out of personal interest in her, interest in the topic, or for some other reason even he didn't understand. But she was grateful; his presence in her life had been invaluable during this last incredibly demanding year.

She didn't know how to read him. He was always there for her: supportive, caring, helping her out where he could. Letting her talk through her doubts and her fears, cheering her on, taking her out when another day in would have driven her straight to crazy.

He was careful, especially since that evening on the deck of the beach house last fall, not to treat her in any way she could construe as romantic. Still…there were times she'd caught him looking at her in a certain way.…

Nothing had changed about her attraction to him, except that now it was based as much in knowledge as it was in fantasy. Getting to know Bronson in the context of her ongoing adoption process had been an eye-opening experience. He was everything she would ever want in a man—except that he had no interest in being a father.

For the long term, she and Bronson clearly weren't compatible. For the short term—

Well, he'd been her rock. As much as Mary had been. Bronson had been with her in the process almost from the beginning. She thought again of the gift he'd given her, the porcelain doll she'd named simply Chyna, black-haired and almond-eyed, dressed in red silk pajamas. Red, the color of joy and celebration, he'd told her later.

A china doll to help her keep the faith until the day she held her real China doll in her arms.

Eileen finally got the noisy group settled into chairs. "Congratulations, everyone," she said, beaming. "Give yourselves a hand for all the hard work you've put into this process—you're going to be wonderful parents." When the applause died down she launched into a description of what she called Countdown Phase: what still needed to happen before the child they'd been assigned would legally be theirs, what they needed to do to get ready to travel, what they could expect of their two weeks in China.

"Twenty-three is an unusually large number of assignments to come through at one time," she said. "You'll probably be traveling in two groups on two separate trips, eleven or twelve in each, but we'll have to wait to hear from Beijing to know who goes when."

Eileen passed around some handouts as she talked: instructions for obtaining their visas; a suggested packing list—"Pack light!" she advised; over-the-counter medications they might want to have on hand for minor problems; reminders of immunizations required; travel tips; gift ideas for the orphanage director, the children's caretakers, the local tour guides. "We encourage you to take gifts for the other children in the orphanage as well," she said. "Diapers, clothing, formula, healthy snacks, toys—anything to make their lives a little brighter."

Finally someone asked the question that was uppermost in everyone's mind: "So when do we get to go?"

"Of course at this point, that's up to China."

Groans rose from various places around the room. *More waiting!* Georgine thought, her heart sinking. How long would it take for the CCAA to confirm their travel dates now?

"I know, I know," Eileen consoled them. "If you didn't have patience before you started this process, you've learned it, right?"

"Wrong!" several people answered in unison. Everyone laughed.

"You could be traveling in a month's time," Eileen went on. "On the other hand, we're getting into trade-show time in China in late May, which slows everything down. It may be longer. So pack your bags, get your shots, get your visas—if you have to get them again before you go, better than being unprepared. My best advice is to be ready to travel in early May, but be ready to let your suitcase gather dust by the front door."

"In other words, hurry-up-and-wait," someone piped up from the back of the room. "Again."

"You got it. But you never know. You could be holding that baby in your arms by Mother's Day." She smiled.

Mother's Day! Without thinking, George grabbed Bronson's hand and squeezed it. He absently squeezed back before letting go to scribble more notes on his yellow pad. She pulled her hand away quickly, embarrassed by her spontaneous gesture. Or was she only embarrassed because he hadn't responded with more enthusiasm?

She slanted a look at him, wondering if he was affected by the excitement in the room, wondering how much it mattered to him that she herself was fast approaching the realization of a life-long dream. He suddenly seemed remote, sitting there with his pen and pad, the only one in the room, with the exception of Eileen, not personally affected by the life-changing event the rest of the group was preparing for.

When she hadn't been part of the last group of parents to travel to China, she'd let go of her hope that Bronson would be with her when she picked up her child. But now—possibly—if everything came together just right—

Please, God, she prayed. It would mean so much to have him be there....

"You'll find the Chinese a warm and charming people," Eileen was saying. "But be aware China isn't like the United States. Be prepared to suspend your normal way of operating and do things the way they get done in China. Being direct and demanding isn't going to work. Don't take no for an answer, but remember persistence is the key, not assertiveness. Be willing to wait as long as you have to, and stay polite and courteous throughout the process.

"You might as well not bother to get uptight. You'll be a lot happier if you just go with the flow and let things happen as they happen."

"The woman knows whereof she speaks," Bronson murmured to Georgine. He smiled at her. "Maybe we'll get to go together after all, George."

So he was thinking the same thing! She smiled back.

"The most important thing you can take with you to China," Eileen finished, "more important than your video camera, or hard-sided luggage, or formula, or diapers, or even your underwear, is your good humor. Don't pack it in your luggage—carry it on! Make sure it's always available at a moment's notice. And take special care not to lose it—you'll quite possibly need it more than any other single item you take with you."

Georgine supposed it was a warning that the last part of the adoption process wasn't going to be any easier than the first part had been. But for the life of her, she couldn't imagine being in anything but a good humor when she finally set foot in China. In China, a little girl was waiting for her. *Her* little girl.

Twenty-three

B ronson quietly put himself at Georgine's disposal over the next few weeks. The revisions his editor had requested on Aunt Liddy's book were minimal and quickly dispatched. George, on the other hand, was working long hours at Child's Play, watch-dogging the final phase of the fall catalog production and keeping Kim and Tucker, the new graphic designer, from each other's throats.

He admired her discipline, doing everything necessary to ensure the catalog department would run smoothly after she left at the end of the month, when he knew what she wanted to be doing was shopping and packing and getting her house ready for Suyuan's arrival.

He started at the top of George's Need to Do list, shopping for the baby supplies she needed to take with her. It was an overwhelming experience for a fifty-year-old bachelor; he was completely out of his depth. The number of brands and styles of disposable diapers was staggering, and when he got to the aisle of over-the-counter medications for colds and ear infections and diaper rash he called Mary in bewilderment. "I'm lost in Baby-land—help!"

She was amused. Her little brother, who'd weathered wars and famines and typhoons, completely undone by a shopping trip to the drugstore. "Leave the baby things to me," she soothed. "You can work on that list of gifts for the Chinese officials."

He'd advised George on appropriate gifts to take for the orphanage director, the local guides in the cities they would visit, and the *amahs,* the children's caretakers. Mary was right—the gift list looked much easier to handle.

"Thank goodness she has you," he told his sister fervently.

"Thank goodness she has *you,*" Mary returned, then added, dubiously, "I think."

Bronson felt his hackles rise. Mary knew how to push his buttons. "Meaning?"

"Bronson, you've been wonderful with George through this whole adoption process. But what are you going to do now?"

"What do you mean, what am I going to do? My sabbatical is over at the end of May. I'm going back to work."

"In Hong Kong."

"That's where my job is. Mary, George knows that. She doesn't expect me to be around. It's not as if we have a romance going."

"Tell me you don't love her."

He couldn't, of course. "Love isn't the point."

"Love's always the point."

He was silent.

"How can you just walk out on her and that little girl?"

He was angry with Mary for a week, until he realized he'd been asking himself the same question.

Lord, what would you have me to do? he prayed again.

Follow me, again came the answer.

Can't you be a little more specific? he found himself asking, only half in jest.

He was surprised at the question that occurred to him on the heels of his prayer: *What is it you want, Bronson Bailey?* A question that took him back to the sermon at Depoe Bay Bible Church on the Sunday George had been there with him: *"Delight yourself in the LORD and he will give you the desires of your heart."*

What were the desires of his heart? How could God grant him his desires when he wasn't sure?

You really don't know, Bronson?

He didn't formulate an answer to the question, but he started taking steps to forestall his return to Hong Kong. He didn't want to stay away forever, but he wasn't ready to leave Portland. Wasn't ready to leave Georgine.

Eileen had suggested the parents each send a gift packet to their child in the orphanage, and one Saturday afternoon Bronson whisked George off to Lloyd Center, where they bought paper and crayons, several picture books, and at Bronson's insistence, a Curious George stuffed monkey.

"She won't understand," George said.

"No, but you do. And it's soft and huggable." *Like you*, he almost added. "She'll love it."

They added several pictures of the house and neighborhood and a photo of Georgine, and Bronson stood in line at the post office to send the package off.

Unwilling to ask Mary for any more help, he consulted with his niece Emily about what he could do to "baby-proof" George's house, and spent a day installing bumpers on the sharp edges of the fireplace hearth, safety catches on the cabinet doors, and child gates in strategic locations.

George protested the amount of time he was spending on her errands until he said to her, "I won't be around long after Suyuan gets here. Please—let me do what I can now."

"You've already done so much."

"You've done more than you know for me."

She didn't ask him what, and she let him help her without further objections.

At the end of April Georgine's work as creative director for Child's Play was over. Except for some consulting time over the phone, she'd scheduled the next three months off to be able to spend as much time as possible with Suyuan. Her travel plans, however, still hadn't been approved by the Chinese government. *All dressed up and no place to go,* Bronson thought as he watched her prowl around her house looking for things to do.

The following week, Far East Adoptions offered Bronson a permanent position as escort/interpreter for their Chinese adoption program. The same day, his agent called to tell him she had an offer on his new book proposal.

"You'll never guess," he called to tell Georgine, trying to suppress his excitement. "My publisher is buying your book idea."

"My book idea?" she asked blankly.

"*Letters for a Lifetime.* Based on twenty years of correspondence between Aunt Liddy and her favorite nephew."

"Bronson! That's marvelous! I do get a cut of the royalties?" she teased.

"At least I'll take you out to dinner when I get my advance."

"You'll get it that soon? Before you leave for Hong Kong?"

He took a deep breath. "I'm not going back just yet. I haven't told Stan yet, but I'm leaving the *Examiner.*"

Silence.

"George? Are you there?"

"I'm here. Just—stunned." Another pause. "I had no idea you were thinking about staying, Bron. You haven't said a word."

What was the emotion in her voice? he wondered. Hurt? Confusion? Why?

"I wasn't sure," he said. "I've been praying. The contract offer seems an answer. That and the fact that Far East wants me to keep working for them."

"You mean you'll be with me when I pick up Suyuan after

all? Even if it doesn't happen until June?" This time the emotion in her voice was unmistakable. Her excitement crackled through the receiver. "Oh, Bronson, you don't know—I've so wanted—I can't believe it!"

He laughed at her exuberance. Her response, more than anything, told him he was making the right choice to stay. At least for now.

Midway into May travel approval finally came through from Beijing for the parents of ten children in the group of twenty-three who'd received their child assignments together; they'd be leaving for China in mid-June.

George was not among them.

Two weeks later a second travel date came through, piggy-backing the first. Bronson would meet the second group of parents in Hong Kong's Kai Tak Airport hours after the first group left for the states with their babies.

But the order approved travel for the parents of only another ten children. Georgine and two couples were being left behind.

"I have our contact in Beijing working on it," Eileen assured her. "This has never happened before, that the entire group wasn't allowed to travel together."

Which did nothing to make George feel better. And Bronson, having dealt with China's tortoise-paced bureaucracy for years, held out little hope anything would happen there in time to make a difference for Georgine—an opinion he kept to himself, however. She was disheartened enough as it was.

To keep herself busy—and to convince herself the adoption was really going to happen, he suspected—George contacted the parents of adopted Chinese children in the area and set up several photo sessions. Her results, no surprise to Bronson, were exceptional, and she began picking up other portrait work by word of mouth.

It was one of the hardest things he'd ever done, leaving her at the airport where she'd come to see the first group of parents off to China in mid-June. She looked like a sad little puppy. He wanted to scoop her up and carry her on the plane with him, but he settled for a warm hug and the assurance he'd be praying for her.

"I know you will," she said. "Thanks, Bronson. Take care. I'll see you in a month."

A month was going to feel like an eternity.

The idea came to him on the flight to Beijing. There was something he could do for Georgine while he was in China, something he could send back to her that might make her waiting a little easier.

He had been intrigued from the beginning by Suyuan's name. Long-Cherished Wish. What mother would name her daughter Long-Cherished Wish and then abandon her? What orphanage would give a child such a name?

Even more intriguing, Suyuan's family name was listed as Yin rather than the name of the orphanage, as was normally the case. Moreover, Suyuan's exact birthdate was known. Often birthdates were no more than educated guesses for abandoned children.

It might not be easy tracing Suyuan's history. It might be close to impossible. But information was something Bronson knew how to get. Taking a year off to edit Aunt Liddy's journals wouldn't have dulled the skills he'd honed over almost thirty years.

He'd dealt with the director of the Fuzhou orphanage and his nursing supervisor, Li Jing Mei, on each of his trips to China on behalf of Far East Adoptions. Along with the institution's finance officer, they always accompanied the children to the hotel where the adopting parents waited and participated in the ceremony that transferred care of the babies from orphanage to parents.

He'd established a relationship of sorts with Jing Mei, a woman both competent and compassionate. Perhaps she would be able to help him out. His time would be limited, but after the paperwork required by the Chinese government was completed, before the trip to Guangzhou to process the children's immigrant visas through the U.S. Consulate, his charges had several days of sight-seeing scheduled in Fuzhou. Perhaps he could sneak a couple of hours away without being missed.

At any rate, he was going to try. He had an opportunity to give Georgine a truly wonderful gift.

Twenty-four

"A h yes, Yin Suyuan. She is a special case." The nursing supervisor at the Fuzhou orphanage tapped her pencil against her clipboard. She seemed young to be in such a responsible position, perhaps under thirty, but Bronson knew from his previous encounters with her that she was also bright, articulate, and compassionate.

"You know Suyuan's family name is Yin," Bronson prompted, hoping the obvious comment would elicit further information. He spoke in Mandarin, the official Chinese dialect.

Li Jing Mei hesitated before answering, "It is her mother's name." Then, severely, "Her father does not deserve to have his name attached to her."

"Then she was not abandoned?"

"Ah, but she was." The woman considered Bronson for a moment. "You are a friend of this woman who will be the mother of Suyuan?"

"Yes. Georgine. She's an incredible woman who's been waiting for a long time to have a child to love. Suyuan is lucky."

Jing Mei nodded. "This Georgine is also lucky. Suyuan is a treasure. I myself have fought to keep her." She looked away for a moment, and when her eyes returned to Bronson's face, he saw grief in their depths. "The laws are very strict in China for adoption. We have the same rules that apply for you Americans. Healthy children go to childless singles or couples, thirty-five or older. I have a daughter of my own, born two months after Suyuan."

215

She stopped, searching Bronson's face, as if uncertain whether to continue.

He smelled a story. Could almost taste it as his news-hound instincts kicked in. *Tread lightly,* he cautioned himself as he searched for the right thing to say. *Don't frighten her off. Show her you can be trusted.* "The One-Child Policy is a hardship for you," he tried.

She stiffened, and he thought he'd lost her. *Stupid,* he chastised himself. *You know better than to say anything that could be construed as critical of the government. Even if she agrees, she puts herself at risk to say it.*

"You would like to adopt Suyuan yourself," he tried again.

He thought he'd made another mistake. Not only did her shoulders remain tensed, she looked as if she were about to cry. Just as he had given up hope of getting any more information from her, she spoke.

"Honor demands that I care for the child of my friend," she said, her voice tight. "The state does not allow me."

The child of her friend! Bronson couldn't believe his luck. He was going to coax Suyuan's story out of Jing Mei if it was the last thing he did. Not for himself. For Georgine.

"Don't forget I've seen Suyuan's picture and read her profile," he said gently. "You have been caring for her, Li Jing Mei. You have a part in caring for all these children." He made a sweeping gesture that took in the entire facility as his mind jumped ahead. How much of his own background was he wise to reveal?

"I have been to other child-welfare institutes," he said. "This one is the brightest and cleanest and has the best medical care and the lowest child-to-caretaker rate of any I've seen. Your care is evident in everything you do here, Jing Mei. And finding good homes for your children is another way you show your love for them."

Finally her shoulders relaxed a little. "These are the things I tell myself to fall asleep at night," she said, her expression grateful.

"When Georgine comes for Suyuan, I'll introduce you," he told her. "When she knows how important Suyuan is to you, I know she'll want to stay in touch. She's a photographer—she'll probably send dozens of pictures." He knew George's heart well enough to sense he wasn't speaking out of turn. She'd be thrilled to know her daughter had been not only well-cared-for, but adored. *"Suyuan is a treasure,"* Jing Mei had said.

Something in Bronson's words had won the supervisor over, he realized when she asked if he would like to meet Suyuan.

"I would love to meet Suyuan," he answered, and followed her along a corridor and through a door to a courtyard. "Does she like the monkey Georgine sent?"

Jing Mei laughed. "Like it! Suyuan carries it everywhere."

"I picked it out for her," he said. "His name is Curious George, and he's a character in an American children's book. That's my nickname for Georgine," he added. "Curious George."

"Ah." She looked at him with a gleam of speculation. "You have feelings for this woman, 'Curious George'?"

He hesitated. "She's a very special friend."

"Ah," she repeated, nodding her head. "So maybe Suyuan will have a father."

Bronson would have protested, but he didn't want to say anything to endanger the rapport he was gaining with Jing Mei. He was too close to Suyuan's story now.

Neither did he want to give Jing Mei a false impression by agreeing with her. He held his tongue.

"Chun Hwa," she called across the courtyard. A young woman in her late teens or early twenties looked up from

217

where she played with three toddlers and waved. "My sister," Jing Mei said. "She has been Suyuan's amah for the last ten months. It will be hard for Chun Hwa, too, when Suyuan goes to America."

Another surprise. He was growing more curious by the minute.

Chun Hwa bowed when Jing Mei introduced him but eyed him warily. In one sense, he was the enemy, he realized. Suyuan was clearly adored by these two women, and he represented Suyuan's leaving.

He recognized the little girl immediately, though her picture had not done her justice. She had delicate bones, sparkling brown eyes, hair as black and shiny as a raven's wing. He squatted down to her level. She studied him gravely, clutching the stuffed monkey he had picked out and mailed to her.

"Hello, Suyuan."

Her expression didn't change. What did one say to a child this age? he wondered, suddenly at a loss.

He reached a hand out to the monkey, grabbed its foot, and jiggled it. "Nice monkey you've got there," he said.

A smile lifted the corners of her mouth. Encouraged, Bronson said, "You know what monkeys do, don't you, Suyuan?"

She shook her head, serious again.

"Well...they eat bananas, and they hang by their tails from trees, and they get into lots of mischief. Like you do, I'll bet."

She continued to stare at him solemnly, and suddenly, for reasons he couldn't begin to fathom, it seemed to Bronson that the most important thing in the world at this moment in time was to make Yin Suyuan laugh.

No one was more shocked than he was when in the next moment he began bobbing his head, scratching his armpits, and hooting like a monkey gone berserk.

It worked. Suyuan's eyes rounded in surprise, and then she was giggling. And then she was squealing with laughter. When Bronson lost his balance and fell to his seat on the concrete, she laughed even harder.

Sheepishly, he picked himself up and found the other two toddlers and the two women laughing as well. So much for dignity. What could he do but join in?

"Come to our home tomorrow for dinner," Jing Mei said, as if she had decided in that instant, "and we will tell you all we know of Suyuan."

"Our home" turned out to be a modest apartment Jing Mei shared with her husband, Po Nin Bao, and their little girl. Chun Hwa had joined them for dinner. Bronson recognized how honored he had been to be invited to share a meal in their home. By the end of the evening, he felt even more honored, for he realized they had taken him into their confidence, as if he were a friend and not a stranger.

"My family moved to the village of Maoping in the southern mountains when I was eight," Jing Mei began after putting the baby to bed. "My mother and father were teachers who were transferred from Fuzhou to the countryside. I was angry the government had forced us to move, but my parents told me I must not complain, we were going where we could be most useful.

"I did not know until I met Yin Zhaodi how spoiled I was. I do not mean spoiled in a bad way, like rotten apples. Spoiled in a good way. Treated by my family as if I were important. Valuable. Not second-class because I was a girl, like so many girls in China, even in the city.

"In rural China it was worse than in the city. It is still so. There is a bad name for girls in the countryside, Maggots-in-the-Rice, because the farmers say they eat up the family's resources and give nothing back. 'What good is a daughter?' they say. A girl whose back is not strong enough for the fields, who will require a dowry, who will leave her parents for her husband's family and not be there to take care of them in old age?

"Zhaodi had been made to feel all her life she was a worthless creature. Even the name her mother gave her means 'Bring in a Younger Brother.' A common name in China then, before the One-Child Policy. Only by bearing a son for her husband could a woman prove her value.

"My mother named me Jing—excellent, best quality—and Mei—little sister—because I was the second child, after my brother. Second in place, but not second in esteem. Zhaodi was open eyed with wonder, like a fish, when she learned my name and saw it was true, my family treated me like best quality. And when my little sister was born and we held a full-month ceremony for her, she could not believe it. Full-month ceremonies were for boys!"

"And what did she think of my name?" Chun Hwa asked curiously, as if hearing some of her family story for the first time.

"Ah! That a girl would be named for something as beautiful and sweet as a Spring Flower! She loved you, Chun Hwa. I would get impatient having to watch you, but Zhaodi never tired of you. More than anything she wanted a child of her own, even then."

Turning back to Bronson, she continued, "Zhaodi and I were friends for nine years. Best friends. She was quiet with her family, like a frightened little mouse, and with my parents, too,

220

but alone we talked like magpies, never quiet. Sometimes her questions came like firecrackers, pop-pop-pop, one after another. She wanted to know everything: about the city, how people lived there, what I had done with my friends. I think now that my life was her dream.

"We were seventeen, Zhaodi and I, when the government reassigned my mother and father to Fuzhou. Oh, how we cried! We would write, we said. We would always be friends." She hesitated, then added, "Our children would be friends."

Nin Bao reached to take her hand, a gesture that surprised Bronson. The Chinese couples he had known were reticent to show affection in front of others.

"I went to university and Zhaodi went to work in the rice fields outside Maoping. A waste of her mind, I thought, but she did not complain. What good would it do? China needed farmers. Her family had worked the land for generations. It was an honorable fate.

"I met Nin Bao three years before the minimum age to marry, twenty-five. He was already practicing medicine at the university hospital where I studied for my degree in nursing." She laughed. "He saw, too, that I was 'best value,' and waited for me."

Nin Bao grinned.

"Not long before our marriage," Jing Mei continued, "Zhaodi wrote to me about a farmer from a good family in a neighboring village who was courting her. Three months after Nin Bao and I were married, she wrote again to say that she and Hu Tianqing were now husband and wife. And then I heard no more. Until last year, two days after the lunar new year, when she knocked here at our door."

Her husband took up the story. "She was a sorry sight, I can tell you! Dirty, smelling of the streets, trembling with fatigue.

'Zhaodi!' Jing Mei cried, and then I knew who she was and that she had come all the way from the mountains. She was huge with child, looking as if she might drop her baby right there on our doorstep. Jing Mei was pregnant with our daughter, but not so far along.

"'Don't worry, please!' were the first words from her mouth. 'It is a legal pregnancy. I have brought my birth permit with me. I would never ask you to compromise your safety for an illegal birth, Jing Mei.' Those were her words. Imagine worrying about us when she could hardly stand!"

"That was the way Yin Zhaodi was," Jing Mei interjected. "Always thinking of others."

"Her legs gave way as she stood there," Nin Bao said. "I caught her and helped her reach a chair. And I am afraid I scolded her. 'You must know such arduous travel so close to term is not good for the baby,' I said. But not unkindly." He shook his head in remorse. "She wept as if she would weep forever."

"Ah, Nin Bao, it was not your scolding that made her weep, but the kindness in back of your scolding," Jing Mei comforted him, squeezing his hand.

She took up the story again. "She could not even undress herself, she was that tired. I helped her out of her clothes, and then I discovered the secret she had kept by stopping her letters to me." She winced, as if in pain. "The wounds were old, the stripes had healed, but oh, what a story of horror the scars wrote on her back! I would not hear it from her mouth for another day, for she slept that long.

"The scars were old, she said, only because Tianqing believed his mother's superstitious reckoning that her baby was a boy. Zhaodi was not convinced. 'If I bear a girl,' she said, 'Tianqing will kill her. And then he will beat me so that if I do not die I will wish I had.' Her eyes were like burning coals, rage against her husband and fierce love for the child she carried flaming there. How large with courage her liver had grown since I had seen her last!

"'I will not let him kill my child,' she told me. 'I will not let him hurt me anymore.' She did not ask for help. She knew I would give it, as she would have given me."

Bronson was mesmerized by the story. "So Zhaodi was Suyuan's mother," he said in awe. No wonder Jing Mei felt so protective of the little girl.

"Suyuan was born not two weeks later," Nin Bao said, as if knowing Jing Mei needed time out from the dramatic tale. "Here in this house. She called her only *bao-bao* then—precious baby. 'If heaven does not grow jealous and steal my daughter away before her full-month feast,' she said, 'I will know she is meant for life on this earth. And then I will give her a name.'"

"You delivered the baby?" Bronson asked. He suddenly thought of Aunt Liddy, of all the babies she'd delivered in China. Few of them in a hospital.

"Jing Mei and I," Nin Bao said. "We were afraid her husband would track Zhaodi down if she checked into a hospital. She believed he would never find her at our house; she had covered her tracks well, and though she had talked of Jing Mei when they were courting, she had not mentioned her name since then."

Bronson knew what was coming. "But he found her," he said, his heart sinking.

Nin Bao nodded. "On the very night we gathered to celebrate the baby's full-month feast. Zhaodi had recovered well from the birth. The whole day while we were gone to work, she prepared for the celebration. She made spring rolls and steamed dumplings, prepared rice noodles to bring her child long life, and raw fish for prosperity. She baked the bread, braided into a ring, for the naming ceremony. She boiled eggs and dyed them red for happiness, as gifts for us and for Chun Hwa.

"'So it is only a small celebration,' she told us. 'But someday I will tell my daughter stories of her full-month ceremony, and she will know that she was loved and wanted from the beginning of life.'"

Chun Hwa broke into the story. "The apartment smelled like a little corner of heaven when I arrived," she said. "And filled with happiness as heaven will be. We made ourselves drunk on laughter, and food, and drink. Then Nin Bao and I held up the wreath of bread, and Zhaodi held the baby, saying to her, 'Because I have waited with such patience, I name you Suyuan.' Long-Cherished Wish. And then she passed Suyuan through the ring to Jing Mei as we cried 'Good health! Long life!'"

"And just at the instant Suyuan's weight transferred from Zhaodi's hands to mine," Jing Mei interrupted, "the door from the hallway burst open. I knew it was Tianqing even before Zhaodi said his name."

Suddenly tears were streaming down Jing Mei's cheeks. Nin Bao put his arms around her, pulled her head down on his shoulder, smoothed her hair.

"There was nothing we could have done," he said in a low voice. His eyes met Bronson's. "Like a mad dog Tianqing leapt across the room for Zhaodi's throat, cursing and screaming. 'No one causes me to lose face as you have done,' he roared, shaking her like a sack of grain. 'I am going to kill you, and then I am going to take my son!'"

Jing Mei lifted her head. "I knew he would kill Suyuan, too, when he found she was a daughter and not a son," she said, her voice broken. "I tried to protect her. I tried—"

"There is nothing you could have done," Nin Bao insisted.

"What happened in the next two days, after Tianqing kicked his way out of the apartment with the screaming baby," he explained, "no one will ever know. Within forty-eight hours, Suyuan was discovered unharmed in a cardboard box beneath a table at the Pet Market, still wearing her full-month gown, though it was torn and soiled. No one could say how or when she had arrived there."

"You can imagine my great shock and overwhelming joy when the police delivered Suyuan to the child-welfare institute where I work," Jing Mei said, her voice low but steadier.

"The gods knew you had done your best by her," Nin Bao said quietly. "They brought her back to you."

"And Tianqing?" Bronson prompted.

"The police were waiting in his village when he returned," Jing Mei said. "He will not harm anyone again."

When Bronson left the house that night, he carried with him two gifts for Georgine: Suyuan's story, and the tiny red and yellow silk gown she had worn for her full-month feast, five bats embroidered across its back. Jing Mei had laundered and mended it.

Chinese could be a playful language. Bronson knew the word for bat was pronounced the same as the word for happiness. Five bats. Five blessings. Zhaodi's wish for her child, carefully stitched for all the world to see.

Now, through George, Zhaodi's wish for her daughter's happiness could come true.

Twenty-five

eorgine heard the phone ring as she slipped her key into the lock on the front door. She flung the door open and raced for the kitchen, tossing her purse on a chair as she reached for the receiver. This could be the call! The second group was leaving for China tomorrow—maybe there was still a chance she'd be with them....

"Hello?"

"You're out of breath. Did I make you run?"

"Bronson! Where are you?"

"My hotel room in Hong Kong. George, I couldn't wait to tell you. I tried to call from China, but I couldn't get through. I've met Suyuan!"

"You've met Suyuan! You mean she was there after all? At the hotel in Fuzhou? I was supposed to be on this trip?"

"No, for some reason the paperwork still hasn't come through. I did talk to our contact in Beijing, though, and she's working on it." He paused. "Are you sitting down?"

She settled onto a stool at the kitchen counter, her heart thumping. He sounded excited. "I am now. Bronson, what's going on?"

"I went to the orphanage to see if I could find out something more about Suyuan. I'd been puzzled by a couple of things."

George listened with growing amazement as Bronson related the story he'd heard from Jing Mei, Nin Bao, and Chun Hwa days before.

"That poor woman!" she gasped as he told her of Tianqing's

attack on Zhaodi and Suyuan's kidnapping. "After having endured so much, thinking she and her baby were finally safe…" She paused. If Suyuan had ended up in an orphanage…

"Zhaodi didn't make it, then," she said softly.

"No."

She chewed at her lower lip as Bronson concluded Suyuan's story. Her stomach felt queasy.

"George? Are you still there?"

"I'm here. I'm just—shocked." She paused. "So, Bronson…"

"Yes?"

"Suyuan was fine? He didn't hurt her?"

"Not a scratch. She was still wearing the red and yellow silk gown Zhaodi had made for her full-month feast. A gown Jing Mei gave me to pass on to you, by the way. George, you have no idea how privileged you are."

A gown Suyuan's birth mother had made. Even more incredible, Suyuan's story. And the greatest treasure of all, Suyuan herself. A miracle baby. "I do know," she said. "I do."

"A year ago I would have seen only the tragedy in this story," Bronson mused. "A year ago I would have wondered where God was."

"And now?"

"Now…Now I see that whenever the hand of man was raised against Suyuan, the hand of God was there to keep her safe. The same way he was with Aunt Liddy all those years when China was at war."

"But what about Zhaodi, Bronson? Where was God for her?"

There was a moment of silence at the other end of the line. "I don't know," he finally said. "I only know that evil exists where men make evil choices. But George—hearing Suyuan's story, seeing the kindness of Zhaodi's friends…even in a world of hurt, caring people make a difference when they choose to.

Like you, Georgine. Here you come into Suyuan's life now, another expression of God's loving grace. Evil exists, but so does love."

George sat deep in thought on the kitchen stool for half an hour after she'd hung up the phone. Bronson was right. In choosing to give man free will, God had chosen also to limit his own powers; but through the love and commitment of his people, his power was still available. One person at a time, a hurting world could be healed. A ravaged world could be made beautiful again.

She, an expression of God's grace in Suyuan's life? George knew the truth: Suyuan was an expression of God's grace in hers. With Suyuan he was granting her the desire of her heart. Her own long-cherished wish.

If she'd been on this trip as she'd hoped to be, she marveled, she might never have learned about Suyuan's history. If not for her personal connection with Bronson, she might never have known how loved and nurtured her new daughter had been from her earliest hours. She'd never heard of any other adoptive parents of a Chinese orphan who knew anything at all about their child; she was incredibly privileged.

She was anxious to meet Jing Mei and Nin Bao and Chun Hwa. To thank them. To let them know she would make every effort to stay in touch. But she also knew the meeting would be difficult. They would be saying good-bye to a little girl they loved.

More than anything, she longed to meet Suyuan.

How much more waiting could she bear?

She saw the second group of adoptive parents off at the airport the next day and resigned herself to waiting at least another

229

month before she'd be taking her own trip to China. A few days later she spent the Fourth of July with Mary and her family and some other friends from church.

Chris Castle and Suyuan were almost the same age, she mused as she watched him race around the big backyard, giggling as his father, Keith, chased him in circles. Owen and Julie Lewis's little girl Brittany, at thirteen months just taking her first wobbly steps between her mom and dad, was only four months younger. Beau and Emily's two girls, at three and six, were at an age they'd probably treat Suyuan like a baby doll.

Izzy, too, would be thrilled to have another baby to play with, and even her friend Danny enjoyed the younger children in the group. Thirteen years old, and still eminently likable, George thought wryly. Amazing.

Danny's mother Toni was due with her second child anytime. George was glad she and Toni would be mothers of young children together; they'd both been so involved in work the last few years, they'd drifted apart. Still, Toni was very special to her. Her baby would be her husband Clark's first genetic child; he was as excited as Toni about the impending birth. *Bronson's pretty excited about Suyuan,* she reminded herself, thinking of his phone call. But Bronson was not her husband.

Suyuan would have plenty of playmates.

She just wouldn't have a father.

A fabulous uncle, though, she told herself in an effort to lift her spirits. *Until he finally moves back to Hong Kong.*

The thought didn't cheer her at all.

Watching the fireworks explode over Portland from the upper deck of the stern-wheeler *Snow Swan* on the Willamette River later that evening, with Danny and Izzy clinging to the rail on either side of her, she imagined Suyuan in her arms, clapping and oohing at the spectacular light show. "You were born in the land where fireworks were invented," she would tell her daughter someday.

But Suyuan was not in her arms. Her spirits sank even lower.

Waiting was so hard.

She'd stopped expecting the phone to be the adoption agency, so she didn't know who it was at first when Eileen called the next day.

"Georgine? Did you hear me? Your travel permission came through! We're working on your plane ticket now. How soon can you be ready?"

"Ready? I'm ready!" she whooped.

Except that now, after all her waiting, George was overwhelmed with anxiety that she didn't have enough and she didn't know enough and she really *wasn't* ready.

She thought of a dozen things she hadn't bought that she really needed....

And then her suitcase had to be repacked. And repacked again because the dozen extra items she'd bought took up too much room and she couldn't very well leave out the diapers....

And she'd better take a baby book with her—there was that newest one out she still didn't have....

And she wanted to take extra gifts for Jing Mei and Nin Bao....

And she had to find three thousand dollars in new hundred-dollar bills for the required contribution to the orphanage—a task that took up hours because no one bank had that many hundred dollar bills on hand. "Next time, call a week ahead and order them," she heard from a series of exasperated bankers.

"I didn't know a week ago. I'm going to China to pick up my baby!" Neither their irritation nor her own anxiety could deflate her excitement.

Meanwhile, miraculously, the adoption agency found plane tickets for Georgine and the two couples whose travel dates had been delayed with hers on a flight to Hong Kong and then straight through to Fuzhou, where they would rendezvous with the rest of the group the day before they were scheduled to pick up their babies.

They had forty-eight hours from the first phone call until their plane took off from Portland International Airport. Unfortunately, Georgine's plane tickets arrived by FedEx the afternoon before the scheduled flight while she was out gathering her hundred dollar bills. She knew because they'd left a note that they'd be back the following day. After her flight time!

That little mishap took some scrambling to set to rights, but when the plane lifted off the tarmac, George was aboard.

Fourteen hours later, she was in the airport at Fuzhou, China.

How she longed for the comfort of Bronson's presence—and especially his translating skills—as she and the two couples she'd traveled with stood in line after line after line, changing their dollars into yuan, going through security, paying the airport tax, going through immigration. At each stop the Chinese officials wanted to see their passports, their tickets, their boarding passes, their tax receipts....

When they finally checked in at their luxurious Western-style hotel, the rest of the group had not yet arrived from Beijing. They weren't expected for another four or five hours, the clerk at the front desk informed them. George was tired—but too keyed-up to nap. And hungry—but not for the hamburgers and steaks in the hotel restaurant. One couple decided to stay at the hotel, but George and the other couple opted for adventure: they got on the bus with a pen and pad of paper and found their way around by drawing pictures.

And of course George took her camera. She wanted an album full of pictures to show Suyuan as she grew. "This is the city where you were born...."

In a restaurant where no one in the house spoke a word of English, George's rudimentary drawings got them a delicious meal of spicy chicken and moist fish and steaming rice and vegetables—and, almost, a bowl of squiggling eels. When the eels appeared at the table, she shook her head in horror and hastily redrew her picture to show a stick figure, arms outstretched with lines drawn between the hands. After an excited conversation George could hear from the kitchen, then a burst of laughter, the entire kitchen staff, broad smiles on their faces, appeared moments later with a bowl of noodles.

George tried to put herself in Zhaodi's shoes as they explored the huge city after their meal. Suyuan's mother had been heavy with child at the time she'd arrived in Fuzhou. She had traveled two days from the cool mists of her mountain village to this hot, dirty city with its yellow skies. It must have been overwhelming, trudging along these congested streets with swollen feet, her back undoubtedly aching, her throat closing up against the smog. How hot was Fuzhou in February? Had sweat trickled down her neck the way it now trickled down Georgine's, like insects crawling beneath her clothes?

New construction was underway throughout the city: buildings, roads, bridges, factories. Cars and trucks shared the road with buses, motorcycles, scooters, and countless bicycles. George caught a bicyclist on film weaving through the heavy traffic pulling a cart that balanced two giant sheets of plate glass.

So many buses! So many bicycles! So many people! And it was everybody for himself when the buses stopped and opened their doors, dozens of people swarming up the steps like angry hornets while dozens more swarmed down, nobody giving way. As Westerners, George and her companions were awarded some amount of deference. Had Zhaodi received the same consideration in her advanced stage of pregnancy? Or had she been just another face, just another body in the crowd?

Being one of so many must have made her feel safe, George mused. Even if Tianqing suspected she had come to Fuzhou, how would he find her? She had left no clues about her ties to Jing Mei. The city would swallow her, and Tianqing would be out of her life forever....

Had she been naive, or only blinded by the bright hope of her future? She and Jing Mei had, after all, been best friends for almost a decade in a village just up the mountain from the village where her husband lived. Everyone would have known about their friendship. An angry, determined man would have found his run-away wife. *Did* find her.

By the time they got back to the hotel, George was tempted to go straight to bed. Eileen had given the group of adoptive parents some hints about overcoming jet lag, however, so she and the two couples sat in the hotel lobby drinking coffee to stay awake until the rest of the group arrived from the Beijing portion of their trip. Someday, they all vowed, they would come back to China and see the Great Wall and the Forbidden City—with their daughters.

"What have you named your baby?" one of the wives asked Georgine.

"The name her mother gave her is Suyuan," George replied, and explained the meaning of the name. "I can't imagine a name more suitable, so I'm going to call her Suyuan as well. Her middle name will be Janae. 'God has replied.' She's not only my long-cherished wish, but a long-awaited answer to my prayers."

"Suyuan Janae Nichols," the woman said, nodding. "It has a nice ring. We're keeping our baby's Chinese name as her middle name, but she's going to be Victoria, after my grandmother. Tori."

George spotted Bronson before he saw her, coming through the doors of the hotel lobby in conversation with several people. His eyes lit as they met hers, and he hurried over to greet her little group. "You're here! I was so glad when I got the message at our hotel in Beijing!" He shook hands all around, but for Georgine he had a special greeting—a long, warm, all-encompassing hug. She didn't realize until then how tired and relieved and happy she was, or just how much she'd missed him. She sobbed into his shoulder.

"George, what's wrong?" he asked in alarm, holding her away from him.

She tried to smile through the tears streaming down her cheeks. "Nothing, you big galoot," she finally got out around her sniffles. "I'm just so happy!"

The frown between his brows smoothed as he realized she really was okay, even if she did have the oddest way of showing it.

"I've missed you," she said.

"Ah. So that's why you're calling me a 'big galoot.'"

She laughed.

"How long have you been here?"

"Hours. We thought you'd never arrive."

"Let me get everyone checked in here," he said. "And then I want to hear about everything that's happened since you found out you were going to get to join the group."

It was after midnight before he left her at the door to her room. He smiled down into her eyes as he said good-night, and when his eyes flickered to her lips, she thought for a moment he was going to kiss them.

Instead he pulled her into his arms and laid his head against her shoulder. "It's a very emotional time," he said. "Try to get a good night's sleep."

He's talking to himself, she thought as she closed her door. *"It's a very emotional time, Bronson Bailey. Don't get carried away. Don't do something you're going to regret in the morning."*

For a moment, she felt a wave of longing. He'd been such an important part of her life these last sixteen months. Why couldn't he want to stay with her always? To share in this miracle that was happening to her?

To be part of the miracle himself?

Twenty-six

ronson had been through this part of the process with groups of adopting parents half a dozen times by now for Far East Adoptions. But he had never felt the way he felt this morning. As nervous and excited as the ten couples and three single women who milled about the room, waiting to meet their daughters for the very first time.

He didn't ask himself why. He wasn't ready for the answer.

Suddenly the door to the hotel conference room opened. He stepped forward to greet the two men who entered—the director of the orphanage and the "finance minister," the official who would collect the adopting parents' contributions to the institution. Jing Mei followed. The door closed behind them, but not before the sounds of wailing could be heard from the hallway. Bronson could feel the tension in the room notch up.

Bowing to each of the Chinese officials and then shaking hands with each, he made his official speech to them as representative of the adoption agency, then handed the finance minister the envelope filled with the collected contributions. The orphanage director thanked them all, "on behalf of every child who will benefit from your generosity," and made his own official welcoming speech, which Bronson dutifully translated.

Jing Mei walked to the door and reopened it. The noise level in the hallway had increased. Thirteen amahs trailed into the room, each cradling a child, most of them between the ages of six and nine months. All of the babies and most of the young women were crying. Seeing Chun Hwa holding Suyuan at the end of the line, tears streaming down both their cheeks and Suyuan clutching her stuffed monkey, Bronson felt his heart constrict.

He'd always looked at this event from the adopting parents' point of view, where the tears were tears of joy. Since hearing Suyuan's story from Chun Hwa and Jing Mei and her husband, he had a new perspective. These amahs were giving up children they had grown to love, children who had formed attachments to them. Turning them over to strangers who could give them opportunities they would never have in China now seemed to him the ultimate gift of love and faith.

One by one, as Bronson called the names of the adopting parents, Jing Mei lifted the children from the arms of their amahs and introduced them by their Chinese names. "Please take your baby," she finished in Mandarin, transferring each little girl to her new parents' arms as Bronson repeated her words in English.

"It's a very good sign they're crying," he heard one of the new mothers, a woman he'd learned was a child psychologist, say in a low voice to someone standing nearby. "Both the babies and the nannies. These children have been loved."

Georgine and Suyuan were the last to meet, and by that time, the rest of the room was buzzing with noise as the parents and their babies got acquainted. Several children were still howling, but others had settled down.

"Georgine Nichols," he said, meeting her eyes. He watched with pride as she stepped forward, thinking about all the effort she'd put into reaching this place, all the insecurities she'd suffered and all the sacrifices she'd made. All the effort and insecurity and sacrifices she was committing herself to for the rest of her life. Her face glowed and her eyes shone with excitement and love for this child she had yet to hold in her arms. He thought he had never seen anyone so radiantly beautiful in all his life.

Jing Mei lifted the sobbing Suyuan from her sister's arms. "Yin Suyuan," she said, not meeting Georgine's eyes, her voice cracking. She did not immediately say, "Please take your baby," as she had with each of the other children. Instead, she buried her face in the little girl's hair and spoke in words Bronson could barely hear above the din in the room.

"I will always hold you in my heart, Yin Suyuan. Do not forget your Auntie Jing Mei. I was the best friend I knew how to be to the mother who bore you, who loved you beyond the stars in the sky."

Suyuan settled against Jing Mei's shoulder, calmed by her familiar voice. "May you live a long life filled with riches and tranquillity," Jing Mei continued softly. "May you learn to love virtue, and at the end of your life, may you look back and see only the happiness."

George was jittery with nerves. She'd recognized Suyuan at once; after all, she'd been looking at her picture every day for the last three months. She was also the only child of toddler age in the group—and she was carrying the Curious George monkey Bronson had insisted they send to her.

But instead of the sweet, mischievous smile she'd gotten used to from the photograph, the expression on Suyuan's face was one of abject misery. Like the younger babies, she'd been sobbing since before her amah had walked into the room with her. It didn't help that the nanny was in tears herself.

George knew from Bronson's description this must be Chun Hwa, and the woman who was transferring each baby from amah to adopting parent on behalf of the orphanage was her sister Jing Mei, the friend of Suyuan's birth mother. How difficult this must be for them! To have to say good-bye to this beautiful little girl they'd loved since the day of her birth. No wonder Chun Hwa was crying. No wonder Jing Mei's expression as she held Suyuan was so forlorn.

She knew without needing translation that Jing Mei was telling Suyuan good-bye. But she had waited so long for this moment. Not just the three months since she'd received her child assignment. Not just the fifteen months since she'd applied to the adoption agency. All her life.

Bronson said something to the woman in Chinese. She looked at George and nodded. George touched his sleeve. "What, Bronson? What did you tell her?"

"I told her you were the friend I had talked about, Suyuan's new mother, and that you had prayed for many years for a child to love. I told her you would be good to Suyuan."

"And what did she say?"

He smiled. "She told me that your eyes are kind."

George smiled warmly at Jing Mei and bowed her head in acknowledgment. "Tell her how grateful I am for the love she has given Suyuan," she said to Bronson. "Tell her I am in her debt. Tell her Suyuan will grow up hearing about her Auntie Jing Mei in China. Tell her I will bring her back someday."

At the sound of her name, Suyuan raised her head and turned to look at George with her dark eyes. Bronson rattled off several Chinese phrases, and Jing Mei nodded and returned her smile, though it was tremulous.

George suddenly remembered the story in Bronson's "Gone Missing" article about Peanut, the little girl who in her short life had known only a few brief hours of affection—not enough to save her. *Thank you, God, for giving Suyuan loving arms to hold her all along her journey,* she prayed. *Return such love and grace to Jing Mei and her family a hundredfold. I can never repay her.*

Jing Mei turned Suyuan around in her arms to face

Georgine and said something to the little girl. George recognized the English "mama" in her words.

Suyuan stared at George solemnly, but when Jing Mei said, "Please take your baby," and passed her into George's waiting arms, her body went rigid and she began to wail again.

George was stunned by the intensity of the pain she felt in that moment, like a knife twisting in her heart. She'd been warned to anticipate the absolute worst on meeting her child, knew this initial rejection was common for adopted children when they were torn away from everything familiar in their lives. But she must not have believed it would happen with Suyuan. Not after waiting so long. Not when God had been with her all along the way.

Certainly she'd had no idea how unimaginably hurtful it was going to feel.

She bounced Suyuan in her arms, spoke soothingly, then cheerfully, then started to hum. She tried a little dance, singing and swaying and turning in a circle, all the while telling herself, *This is common, don't take it personally, she'll figure out before long that you love her....*

Nothing seemed to help ease either Suyuan's misery or George's.

Jing Mei looked distressed as the toddler stretched her arms out to her, crying pitifully, but she shook her head in sorrow. She pointed at Georgine and said again in English, "Mama!"

"George, let me try."

Startled, she swung her head around to meet Bronson's eyes. Had she heard him right?

"Let me try," he said again. "Suyuan! Remember me?" He jiggled the foot of the monkey she was now holding by its tail. Suddenly he was hopping around, scratching his armpits and making monkey noises. If George hadn't been so shocked, she

241

would have laughed at the utter astonishment on the faces of the orphanage director and his finance minister. This was not the Bronson Bailey they were accustomed to. Nor she, for that matter.

Suyuan's crying stopped abruptly. Her eyes rounded as she stared at Bronson, and a moment later she was giggling loudly. A beautiful sound, Georgine thought, pleased.

The little girl reached her arms out to him. He met George's eyes. "Okay?" he asked. "Just for a couple of minutes?"

She hesitated, not wanting to let go of Suyuan. This was her daughter, the child she'd been waiting for.

"Maybe if you did the monkey thing," he coaxed. "While I hold her."

Nodding, she let him lift the toddler from her arms. She didn't do his "monkey thing," but she came up with a game of her own, playing peekaboo behind her hands. Every child she'd ever known loved playing peekaboo, and Suyuan proved to be no exception, laughing with delight and even mimicking her actions. But each time Georgine reached for her, she clung to Bronson.

"Mama," he said, pointing to George. "Go to Mama?" *No,* Suyuan shook her head furiously.

You're being silly, George told herself as the hurt welled up again. *She's just a baby, doing what babies do in a new and frightening situation.* But as she already knew, hurt was no respecter of logic.

Bronson ended up holding Suyuan while he translated the adoption contract as the orphanage director read it aloud; she seemed perfectly content with the arrangement.

Although her arms ached to hold her daughter, Georgine tried to concentrate on the formalities, the short, choppy, almost singsong Mandarin and Bronson's deep voice translating the terms of their agreement into English.

The contract seemed odd to her, but it addressed concerns that must be very real to the Chinese: The Americans would not rear their girls to be servants, nor would they abandon them, transfer them to other parents, or force them into arranged marriages. They would care for their new children lovingly and grant them inheritance rights. They would teach them about their heritage. And, if possible, they would bring them back to visit their homeland.

It would be wonderful to bring Suyuan back to China when she was older, she thought. Back to see the friends who had cared for her as if she were their own. To see the wonders of her native land. Bronson had told her last night what she'd missed in the first days of the trip: the Great Wall, Tiananmen Square, the Summer Palace, the Temple of Heaven, the Forbidden City; a cloisonné factory and a silk factory, and a troupe of incredibly agile Chinese acrobats.

She wanted Suyuan to learn about her history and culture, and she wanted to share the experience with her. Maybe when she was four or five, when she was old enough to understand and appreciate what she saw....

If she even likes me by then, she thought morosely, gazing once again at Suyuan in Bronson's arms. She looked so comfortable there. Even more amazingly, Bronson looked comfortable. With a child in his arms!

He turned at that moment and caught her eye. The smile on his face was cheerful, almost gleeful.

George straightened in her chair. He really was going above and beyond the call of duty, she mused. Or was it just duty? She watched thoughtfully as he returned his gaze to Suyuan and tickled her tummy.

Their hotel floor the next few nights felt more like a dormitory, with everyone's doors open and people stopping by each other's rooms constantly to compare notes—some about what sights shouldn't be missed and where to buy the best souvenirs and which restaurants had the tastiest food, but more often about which baby had pooped and how much, and which babies had stayed up all night partying.

"Talk about a sudden change in priorities!" one new father joked after telling a group how many diapers his little girl had already gone through. "Can you imagine this conversation back home in the boardroom?"

The child psychologist in their group assured George that Suyuan would warm up to her. She wasn't the only child in the group who was having trouble adjusting. "The fact that she's grieving means she's attached," she told her. "Which means she's capable of attachment. It's a good thing, Georgine. Give her time."

George knew in her head the woman was right. But in her heart, she was afraid. *Please God,* she prayed. *Let her feel how much I love her.*

They stayed in Fuzhou several days to finalize the paperwork that would ensure the adoptions were legal under Chinese law. Bringing a stroller had been a good idea; Suyuan would have been too heavy to carry around the city, even if she'd allowed it, and she liked to go for rides. George was hoping her good feelings about the stroller would transfer to the woman pushing it.

She honestly didn't know what she'd have done without Bronson, though she felt a little resentful about her dependence on him. Suyuan continued to fuss and cry every time she held her, bathed her, changed her diaper, dressed her, fed her. Only Bronson's presence seemed to calm her. She wouldn't even sleep at night unless he put her down.

Perhaps it was the familiarity of the Chinese words he

244

spoke, or his dark hair, or the fact they'd met under less disruptive conditions than a room full of crying babies and nannies....

Whatever it was, it seemed dreadfully unfair.

Bronson was having the time of his life with Suyuan. She was very bright; she seemed to understand him when he spoke to her in Chinese and listened in wide-eyed interest as he pointed out items and said their names, first in Mandarin and then in English. She was even repeating words back to him.

She ate anything he set in front of her, and as her profile had stated, she really did love to comb her hair and brush her teeth. The world felt new as he explored it through her eyes on their daily journeys into the city. He didn't even mind changing her diapers.

But he hurt for Georgine. More, he felt anxious and guilt stricken that the little girl had taken to him so quickly and not to George, when it was George's heart that had ached for a child so long. He talked about George every day to Suyuan: "Mama loves you. Mama is going to take you home. You'll like Mama's house. Mama's house is Suyuan's house...."

"I know I can't push her, Bronson. I know the only way it's ever going to work is to accept whatever Suyuan is willing to give me until she trusts me enough to give me more. But it's so hard! If only I spoke Chinese, so I could talk to her," she fretted. "I'm so jealous of your—*familiarity.*"

He winced. "Do you want me to back off?"

"No, of course not. At this point, we'd both be lost without you."

We'd both be lost without you....

At this point, he reminded himself. If anyone could make a success of life as a single mother, it was Georgine. Suyuan would come around, and they'd be fine without him.

But would he be fine without Georgine and Suyuan?

"Don't worry about the language, George," he told her, avoiding the question. "She's learning English fast. Besides, the language of love is universal, and you speak love like a native. She'll come around."

"But when?" George's expression was bleak. "Bronson, I've been waiting so long."

"I know you have," he said, stroking her cheek tenderly. "I know."

He couldn't think of anything else to say.

Twenty-seven

'm wasting my trip to China.

Georgine woke with the thought very early the morning before the adoption group was to leave Fuzhou for Guangzhou, where the immigration paperwork for the babies would be finalized with the American Consulate.

She was worrying about things over which she had no control, she realized, and not taking advantage of the fact she was in the midst of a culture that had fascinated her for years. And hadn't she brought her camera so she'd have pictures to show Suyuan her birthplace? She hadn't taken a photo since her first afternoon in the city.

Looking out her window, she saw a group of people practicing *tai chi* in the park across the street as morning light stole across the sky. She checked on Suyuan in the crib at the end of the bed. Still sleeping. She reached down to stroke her cheek, gently, pain for her daughter's continued rejection mixed with her joy and love. *How much longer, God? I thought my waiting was over....*

She walked to the window again. The slow, synchronized movements of the group in the park were almost hypnotic. As she watched them, George made a decision: she would make the best of the time she had left in China, and she would leave Suyuan in God's hands—where she had belonged from the beginning.

Dressing hurriedly, she slipped her camera around her neck and, leaving her own door open, crept down the hall to knock lightly on Bronson's door. If he didn't answer, she'd just have to miss this particular photo opportunity. That was all right—she would make others. But if he happened to be up, maybe he'd be willing to watch Suyuan for a little while....

The door opened, and, in fact, Bronson looked as if he'd been up for hours. The screen of his laptop computer, set up at the desk in his room, was lit. Did the man know the meaning of *relax*?

About like you do, came the answer.

"George? Is everything all right? Where's Suyuan?" He sounded alarmed.

"Everything's fine. I just thought—but I see you're busy. Never mind."

He glanced at the camera around her neck. "You want to take some pictures. George, I think that's great." He grinned. "Never thought I'd say such a thing, but I'd be happy to baby-sit. Take as much time as you want."

Taking a couple of hours off from the intense emotion of the last few days was the best thing she could have done. Both for herself and for Suyuan, as it turned out.

By the time she returned to her hotel room, she'd taken three rolls of film of the tai chi practitioners in the park; dancers practicing the two-step and the fox-trot in the hotel parking lot; and a stream of food vendors on their way to set up at the outdoor market, some with collapsible booths and already-burning cooking fires strapped to their bicycles. The day began early in Fuzhou.

She kept her camera with her for the rest of the day, letting Bronson manage Suyuan in the stroller while she captured images of China: the Buddhist monks at Drum Mountain, the giant panda at the zoo, exotic birds and fish and turtles for sale at the Pet Market. And everywhere, people: shoppers and shopkeepers, grandmothers, schoolgirls, and babies, men and women dressed in traditional Chinese tunics and trousers or in modern Western clothing.

And, of course, her camera turned often to her daughter, who showed great interest in the instrument and what Georgine was doing with it. Perhaps Suyuan thought it was another version of her favorite peekaboo game. At any rate, for once she didn't seem to mind being the focus of George's attention.

Georgine was more relaxed and had more fun that day than she'd allowed herself since she'd arrived in China. Maybe Suyuan sensed it and relaxed as well. Or maybe God had been waiting for George to turn her anxiety about Suyuan over to him.

For whatever reason, when it was time for bed later in the evening, Suyuan let George bathe her alone while Bronson made some phone calls from his room. By the time he came back, they were sitting on the bed, Suyuan in a soft PlayBabies sleeper, sitting on George's lap while she read one of her favorite children's books, *The Runaway Bunny.*

Georgine had no idea if Suyuan understood a word, but she listened quietly all the way to the end and communicated clearly that she wanted to hear it a second time through.

George happily obliged, this time inserting Suyuan's name into the story and identifying the mother bunny as "Suyuan's mama."

As she finished reading, with Bronson looking quietly on from a chair across the room, Suyuan pointed to the last page. "Soon mama," she said.

"Yes! Suyuan's mama."

As George closed the book, Suyuan yawned and snuggled against her, not resisting the arms that tightened around her. Bronson quietly brought the bottle of formula from the hotpot where George had been warming it.

Suyuan leaned to one side and stared solemnly up into Georgine's face. George held her breath as she lifted her tiny hand and touched her cheek. "Soon mama," she said again. A moment later she was drinking from her bedtime bottle as she continued to gaze into her new mother's face, intently, as if memorizing its features.

Another five minutes and she was asleep.

An angel, George thought as she cradled her sleeping child in her arms. *My long-cherished wish.*

Tears coursed down her cheeks, washing away her pain and leaving inexpressible joy in their wake.

Although he had official duties to perform as he shepherded the new parents through the final phase of the adoption process in Guangzhou, Bronson was never far from George and Suyuan. He knew George could take care of herself, and Suyuan no longer let her mother out of her sight, but he felt protective.

Tall, blond Georgine drew even more attention from the Chinese than the other Americans did. One woman wanted to know if she was Russian, and another if she was a movie star. For the most part she handled their curiosity with grace, but one time he saw the horrified look on her face when the local guide translated a question from an elderly Chinese woman: "Are you taking this baby home to perform medical experiments on her?"

"Tell her I am taking this baby home because she is my daughter and I love her," she instructed the guide. Later she told Bronson she'd thought about replying, "Experiments? Suyuan is the one performing experiments—on me!"

"I wasn't sure the humor would translate," she said.

"Good call," he said, grinning, then added, "After a rocky start, her experiments seem to be working out quite well."

"Yes, they are. She's going to make a parent of me yet!"

Bronson had tried to reach Pamela in Hong Kong from the hotel in Fuzhou and finally managed to get through from their luxurious five-star Guangzhou hotel, the White Swan. He made arrangements to meet her for coffee the last morning the group would be in Hong Kong.

He'd written Pamela once since he'd run into her in March, telling her he'd decided to stay in Portland a while longer. He'd told her about the new book, and the long-term position with Far East Adoptions. He hadn't told her anything about Georgine; he hadn't known what to say.

Do you now? he asked himself.

He had to admit he didn't. But it was time to tell Pamela something. And hadn't God promised to guide him?

Their last night in Hong Kong, he arranged for a final banquet for the new parents and their babies at a local restaurant he'd frequented for years. The Chinese friend who owned it thought he was joking when he made the reservations for twenty-four adults and thirteen children. He raised a skeptical eyebrow. "Children? You? Thirteen? Ah, Mr. Bailey! I suppose you are going to tell me one of them is yours?"

He was almost sorry to have to say none of them were.

He was thinking about the banquet the next morning as he waited for Pamela in the hotel coffee shop. About how much he'd enjoyed dining with a baker's dozen of babies. He grinned as he remembered Suyuan's delight with her Cheerios and fruit while her mother feasted on Peking duck and cashew chicken and moo shu pork. There was something of delight in everything Suyuan did. It was catching.

"You look happy this morning. Thinking about me?"

He rose to pull out Pamela's chair. "Good morning! Thinking about babies, actually. Sorry."

She threw him an odd look. "Babies! Is there something you haven't told me, Bronson?" she teased.

He looked at her squarely. "As a matter of fact, there is."

Georgine was surprised when Bronson didn't show up for Suyuan's morning feeding. He'd been coming by every morning, even after Suyuan's change of heart toward her mother, when his presence didn't feel quite so essential.

That was all going to change very soon, of course, although George had tried not to think about it. Maybe Bronson was getting them prepared for real life in Portland, when he wouldn't be just down the hall at her beck and call as he'd been for the last week. A week! Was that all the time it had been?

A week, and she was a completely different person. Leading a completely different life. She was Suyuan's *mother.*

Bronson, on the other hand, was still Bronson. Softer, maybe. More tender than she'd expected. But he was not Suyuan's father.

The thought made her very sad. And her sadness made her angry.

Why had he made himself so indispensable, anyway? When he knew he wasn't going to be around for the long run? The jerk.

And why had she let him *become* so indispensable?

"Mama!"

George smoothed her puckered brow and finished cutting up a dried fig in Suyuan's morning bowl of warm rice *congee.* "Comin' up, kiddo! We don't need ol' Bronson around anyway, do we? We're going to be fine, you and me. Didn't God promise to be a father to the fatherless?" She set the bowl on the desk and lifted Suyuan out of her crib. "How about a husband to the husbandless? Isn't that in there somewhere, too?"

"Bon," Suyuan said, which was as much as she could manage of Bronson's name.

Suyuan was fed, changed, and dressed, and George's fit of temper had flared and died by the time Bronson came knocking at their door.

How could she blame him for jumping in to help when she truly had needed him? He'd been wonderful. And the fact was, she didn't need him anymore.

"Good morning!" he said cheerfully, lifting Suyuan from the crib where George had left her to play while she finished up the last of her packing.

"Bon!" Suyuan said happily.

George's heart sank. Maybe they didn't *need* him, need him. But Suyuan was going to miss having him around.

And so was she.

"I've been thinking," Bronson said, taking the chair at the desk and setting Suyuan on his knee. He bounced her up and down. She squealed with delight.

"Oh?" George said, not looking at him as she continued to fold clothes and place them in her suitcase. But her heartbeat quickened. "What about?"

"My next book. After *Letters for a Lifetime,* I mean."

"Oh." Disappointment, which told her she was still dreaming. *Get a grip, Georgine,* she reproved herself. What had she expected? After all, why shouldn't he be thinking about his next book? The next phase in his life. Like Suyuan was the next phase in hers.

"I thought I'd make it a love story."

"A love story!"

"Didn't you recommend once that I write a romance novel?" Bronson asked, his expression innocent. "I've got this character in mind—a crusty, burned-out old bachelor who definitely doesn't want kids. Then he meets this *great* woman—smart, pretty, warm, funny—who turns his heart inside out. But she's crazy about kids."

"Bronson—"

"Wait! Let me finish. Our hero can't help himself. He falls in love. And it changes his whole life. He sees himself with different eyes. He sees the world with different eyes. And then the real miracle—he falls in love with a little girl the heroine's invited into her life. And he realizes he doesn't want to live without them. Without either of them."

At that he wrapped his arms around Suyuan in a bear hug. She giggled.

Bronson looked at George expectantly. "Well? What do you think?"

Joy began to bubble up from some deep reservoir inside her. Joy and a certain sense of mischief he sometimes brought out in her.

"Good premise," she said seriously. "But I don't think it's quite there yet...."

"Not quite *there*," he protested. "What do you mean? It's a great plot! What else does it need?"

"Your hero realizes he doesn't want to live without this woman and this child, right?"

"Right!"

"Well?"

"Well what?"

"Well, what does he do about it?"

Bronson smiled. "I see your point. Our hero has to take

254

some action here to compel the resolution. How's this?"

He turned Suyuan around to face him. "Suyuan, would you let me be your papa?"

"Bon!" Suyuan said, laughing.

"Yes," he agreed. "Bon. Bon be Soon papa?"

George couldn't help herself. She burst into laughter. Mandarin Chinese, yes. Cantonese. Maybe even French. But never in all her life had she ever expected to hear Bronson Bailey speaking Baby.

He cast her an injured look.

"Bon be Soon papa?" he asked Suyuan again.

"Papa!"

"Whew!" he said, wiping his brow. "The kid had me sweating bullets there." Suyuan squirmed in his arms and he set her down. She spotted her stuffed monkey on the floor under her crib and went after it.

"The question now," Bronson continued, "is how our heroine will respond to the other half of our hero's question: Georgine Nichols, will you marry me?"

George frowned. "You're definitely getting there, Bronson, but I feel as if something's still missing...."

"You think so?" There was a sudden, dangerous light in his eyes as he rose from the chair. "How about this version?"

He swept her into his arms and kissed her soundly. Really kissed her. Didn't pull away, and might not have, she suspected, except that Suyuan wrapped an arm around one of her legs and one of his and said with animation, "Mama! Papa!"

Laughing, Bronson lifted the little girl into their combined embrace. Suyuan giggled.

"Georgine Nichols, in you I have found my perfect match. You are *shiquan shimei*, my everything, complete and wonderful. I love you, and I love your daughter. Will you marry me?"

She couldn't even tell him he'd gotten it right, it was the perfect ending to his story. She was crying too hard. True to form.

So she kissed him.

"I'm going to take that as a yes," he said, and kissed her back. Suyuan, anxious to get in on the action, nuzzled her face between them, and suddenly George was laughing through her tears.

So miracles still happened, she thought.

She wrapped her arms around them both and laughed and cried.

Miracles still happened. Here she held them in her arms.

Dear Reader,

An interesting relationship exists between a writer and the characters she creates. Where does one end and the other begin? The line blurs.

My characters are drawn from my experience and reflect my own very personal feelings, perceptions, and beliefs. They are not only my creations; they are, in a certain sense, *me*. Although George and Bronson's experiences are not my specific experiences, their hearts are my heart: their grief and their joy, their confusion and their clarity, their fears and their tenacity, their struggles to understand their place in the world and to answer God's call "to love and to serve."

Thank you for inviting George, Bronson, Zhaodi, Suyuan, and the other characters who live in the pages of this book into your life. Thank you for inviting me! My prayer is that you've discovered something of your own heart in the hours we've spent together.

From my heart to yours,

Barbara Jean Hicks

PALISADES...PURE ROMANCE

∼ PALISADES ∼

Reunion, Karen Ball
Refuge, Lisa Tawn Bergren
Torchlight, Lisa Tawn Bergren
Treasure, Lisa Tawn Bergren
Chosen, Lisa Tawn Bergren
Firestorm, Lisa Tawn Bergren
Surrender, Lynn Bulock
Wise Man's House, Melody Carlson
Heartland Skies, Melody Carlson
Cherish, Constance Colson
Chase the Dream, Constance Colson
Angel Valley, Peggy Darty
Sundance, Peggy Darty
Moonglow, Peggy Darty
Promises, Peggy Darty
Memories, Peggy Darty
Remembering the Roses, Marion Duckworth
Love Song, Sharon Gillenwater
Antiques, Sharon Gillenwater
Texas Tender, Sharon Gillenwater
Secrets, Robin Jones Gunn
Whispers, Robin Jones Gunn
Echoes, Robin Jones Gunn
Sunsets, Robin Jones Gunn
Clouds, Robin Jones Gunn
Waterfalls, Robin Jones Gunn
Coming Home, Barbara Jean Hicks
Snow Swan, Barbara Jean Hicks
China Doll, Barbara Jean Hicks
Angel in the Senate, Kristen Johnson Ingram
Irish Eyes, Annie Jones

Father by Faith, Annie Jones
Irish Rogue, Annie Jones
Glory, Marilyn Kok
Sierra, Shari MacDonald
Forget-Me-Not, Shari MacDonald
Diamonds, Shari MacDonald
Stardust, Shari MacDonald
Westward, Amanda MacLean
Stonehaven, Amanda MacLean
Everlasting, Amanda MacLean
Kingdom Come, Amanda MacLean
Betrayed, Lorena McCourtney
Escape, Lorena McCourtney
Dear Silver, Lorena McCourtney
Forgotten, Lorena McCourtney
Enough! Gayle Roper
The Key, Gayle Roper
Voyage, Elaine Schulte

⟶ ANTHOLOGIES ⟵

A Christmas Joy, Darty, Gillenwater, MacLean
Mistletoe, Ball, Hicks, McCourtney
A Mother's Love, Bergren, Colson, MacLean
Silver Bells, Bergren, Krause, MacDonald
Heart's Delight, Ball, Hicks, Noble
Fools for Love, Ball, Brooks, Jones

THE PALISADES LINE

Look for these new releases at your local bookstore. If the title you seek is not in stock, the store may order you a copy using the ISBN listed.

Heartland Skies, Melody Carlson
ISBN 1-57673-264-9

Jayne Morgan moves to the small town of Paradise with the prospect of marriage, a new job, and plenty of horses to ride. But when her fiancé dumps her, she's left with loose ends. Then she wins a horse in a raffle, and the handsome rancher who boards her horse makes things look decidedly better.

Memories, Peggy Darty
ISBN 1-57673-171-5

In this sequel to *Promises,* Elizabeth Calloway is left with amnesia after witnessing a hit-and-run accident. Her husband, Michael, takes her on a vacation to Cancún so that she can relax and recover her memory. What they don't realize is that a killer is following them, hoping to wipe out Elizabeth's memory permanently....

Remembering the Roses, Marion Duckworth
ISBN 1-57673-236-3

Sammie Sternberg is trying to escape her memories of the man who betrayed her, and she ends up in a small town on the Olympic Peninsula in Washington. There she opens her dream business—an antique shop in an old Victorian—and meets a reclusive watercolor artist who helps to heal her broken heart.

Waterfalls, Robin Jones Gunn
ISBN 1-57673-221-5

In a visit to Glenbrooke, Oregon, Meredith Graham meets movie star Jacob Wilde and is sure he's the one. But when Meri puts her foot in her mouth, things fall apart. Is isn't until the two of them get thrown together working on a book-and-movie project that Jacob realizes his true feelings, and this time he's the one who's starstruck.

China Doll, Barbara Jean Hicks
ISBN 1-57673-262-2

Bronson Bailey is having a mid-life crisis: after years of globetrotting in his journalism career, he's feeling restless. Georgine Nichols has also reached a turning point: after years of longing for a child, she's decided to adopt. The problem is, now she's fallen in love with Bronson, and he doesn't want a child.

Angel in the Senate, Kristen Johnson Ingram
ISBN 1-57673-263-0

Newly elected senator Megan Likely heads to Washington with high hopes for making a difference in government. But accusations of election fraud, two shocking murders, and threats on her life make the Senate take a backseat. She needs to find answers, but she's not sure who she can trust anymore.

Irish Rogue, Annie Jones
ISBN 1-57673-189-8

Michael Shaughnessy has paid the price for stealing a pot of gold, and now he's ready to make amends to the people he's hurt. Fiona O'Dea is number one on his list. The problem is, Fiona doesn't want to let Michael near enough to hurt her again. But before she knows it, he's taken his Irish charm and worked his way back into her life...and her heart.

Forgotten, Lorena McCourtney
ISBN 1-57673-222-3

A woman wakes up in an Oregon hospital with no memory of who she is. When she's identified as Kat Cavanaugh, she returns to her home in California. As Kat struggles to recover her memory, she meets a fiancé she doesn't trust and an attractive neighbor who can't believe how she's changed. She begins to wonder if she's really Kat Cavanaugh, but if she isn't, what happened to the real Kat?

The Key, Gayle Roper
ISBN 1-57673-223-1
On Kristie Matthews's first day living on an Amish farm, she gets bitten by a dog and is rushed to the emergency room by a handsome stranger. In the ER, an elderly man in the throes of a heart attack hands her a key and tells her to keep it safe. Suddenly odd accidents begin to happen to her, but no one's giving her any answers.

ANTHOLOGIES

Fools for Love, Ball, Brooks, Jones
ISBN 1-57673-235-5
By Karen Ball: Kitty starts pet-sitting, but when her clients turn out to be more than she can handle, she enlists help from a handsome handyman.
By Jennifer Brooks: Caleb Murphy tries to acquire a book collection from a widow, but she has one condition: he must marry her granddaughter first.
By Annie Jones: A college professor who has been burned by love vows not to be fooled twice, until her ex-fiancé shows up and ruins her plans!

Heart's Delight, Ball, Hicks, Noble
ISBN 1-57673-220-7
By Karen Ball: Corie receives a Valentine's Day date from her sisters and thinks she's finally found the one...until she learns she went out with the wrong man.

By Barbara Jean Hicks: Carina and Reid are determined to break up their parents' romance, but when it looks like things are working, they have a change of heart.

By Diane Noble: Two elderly bird-watchers set aside their differences to try to save a park from disaster but learn they've bitten off more than they can chew.

BE SURE TO LOOK FOR ANY OF THE 1997 TITLES
YOU MAY HAVE MISSED:

Surrender, **Lynn Bulock** (ISBN 1-57673-104-9)
Single mom Cassie Neel accepts a blind date from her children for her birthday.

Wise Man's House, **Melody Carlson** (ISBN 1-57673-070-0)
A young widow buys her childhood dream house, and a mysterious stranger moves into her caretaker's cottage.

Moonglow, **Peggy Darty** (ISBN 1-57673-112-X)
Tracy Kosell comes back to Moonglow, Georgia, and investigates a case with a former schoolmate, who's now a detective.

Promises, **Peggy Darty** (ISBN 1-57673-149-9)
A Christian psychologist asks her detective husband to help her find a dangerous woman.

Texas Tender, **Sharon Gillenwater** (ISBN 1-57673-111-1)
Shelby Nolan inherits a watermelon farm and asks the sheriff for help when two elderly men begin digging holes in her fields.

Clouds, **Robin Jones Gunn** (ISBN 1-57673-113-8)
Flight attendant Shelly Graham runs into her old boyfriend, Jonathan Renfield, and learns he's engaged.

Sunsets, **Robin Jones Gunn** (ISBN 1-57673-103-0)
Alissa Benson has a run-in at work with Brad Phillips, and is more than a little upset when she finds out he's her neighbor!

Snow Swan, **Barbara Jean Hicks** (ISBN 1-57673-107-3)
Toni, an unwed mother and a recovering alcoholic, falls in love for the first time. But if Clark finds out the truth about her past, will he still love her?

Irish Eyes, **Annie Jones** (ISBN 1-57673-108-1)
Julia Reed gets drawn into a crime involving a pot of gold and has her life turned upside down by Interpol agent Cameron O'Dea.

Father by Faith, **Annie Jones** (ISBN 1-57673-117-0)
Nina Jackson buys a dude ranch and hires cowboy Clint Cooper as her foreman, but her son, Alex, thinks Clint is his new daddy!

Stardust, **Shari MacDonald** (ISBN 1-57673-109-X)
Gillian Spencer gets her dream assignment but is shocked to learn she must work with Maxwell Bishop, who once broke her heart.

Kingdom Come, **Amanda MacLean** (ISBN 1-57673-120-0)
Ivy Rose Clayborne, M.D., pairs up with the grandson of the coal baron to fight the mining company that is ravaging her town.

Dear Silver, **Lorena McCourtney** (ISBN 1-57673-110-3)
When Silver Sinclair receives a letter from Chris Bentley ending their relationship, she's shocked, since she's never met the man!

Enough! **Gayle Roper** (ISBN 1-57673-185-5)
When Molly Gregory gets fed up with her three teenaged children, she announces that she's going on strike.

A Mother's Love, **Bergren, Colson, MacLean**
(ISBN 1-57673-106-5)
Three heartwarming stories share the joy of a mother's love.

Silver Bells, **Bergren, Krause, MacDonald**
(ISBN 1-57673-119-7)
Three novellas focus on romance during Christmastime.